Contributions to our knowledge of the plankton of the Faeroe Channel

G Herbert 1861-1940 Fowler

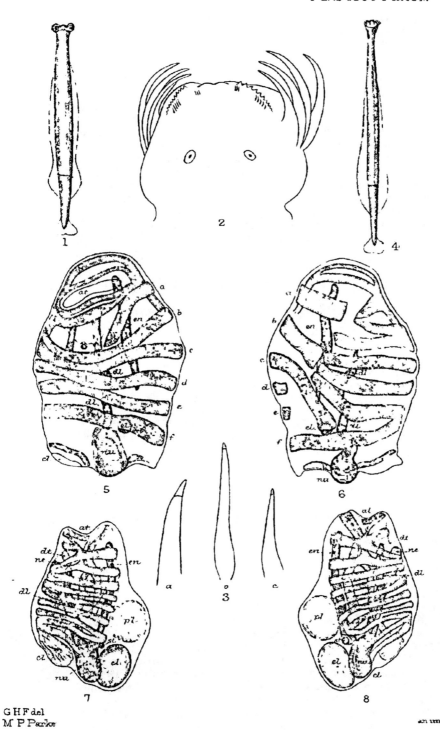

G H F del
M P Parker

an imp

in this country, and Mr. Rothschild has stated (Avifauna of Laysan, p 97) that Lafresnaye's type is in the Paris Museum. On this point he must have been misinformed, and the specimen he "carefully examined" there was probably one of the pair obtained and presented by Néboux (Revue Zoologique, 1840, p. 289), from which presumably the figures in the Voyage of the 'Vénus' (Ois. pl. i. figs. 1, 2) were taken. It is almost needless to remark that had the present example been attainable by Mr. Wilson he would never have supposed it to be specifically identical with the bird which he found in Hawaii; and I may observe that not one of the five examples of the *Hemignathus lucidus* of Oahu at his disposal— two from Berlin, two at Cambridge, and one in the British Museum—was that of a male in full plumage.

Mr. W. B Tegetmeier, F.Z.S., exhibited an interesting application of the Röntgen rays to ornithology, in the shape of an actinograph taken from a Partridge that had "towered" on being shot. The actinograph seemed to show that the "towering" was caused by injury done to the lungs, and not by lesion of the brain, as often supposed.

The following papers were read :—

1. Contributions to our Knowledge of the Plankton of the Faeroe Channel.—No. I. By G. Herbert Fowler, B.A., Ph.D., Assistant Professor of Zoology, University College, London.

[Received November 3, 1896.]

(Plate L.)

Between July 29th and August 8th of this year I enjoyed the great advantage of a berth on H.M.S. 'Research,' by the permission of the Lords Commissioners of the Admiralty, extended to me at the request of the Council of the Royal Society. I am glad of this opportunity to tender my thanks, not only to both of these bodies, but also to Capt. Moore and the other officers of the 'Research' for placing at my disposal every facility that lay in their power.

My chief object on the cruise was an attempt to ascertain whether the intermediate zones of water between (say) 100 and 700 fathoms are characterized by definite forms of planktonic life or not; and if so, what temperature-limits form barriers to the distribution of various species. The large number both of surface and deep-water organisms obtained during the cruise will demand so long a study that it seems best to publish results as soon as obtained in the scant leisure of which a teaching post admits. The present note forms, therefore, the first of a series, in which the methods employed and the general questions of distribution will be left to the last paper.

SAGITTA WHARTONI, sp n.[1]   (Plate L. figs. 1–3.)

In external form this species resembles most nearly *S. lyra* (Krohn), and differs from all other species yet described in the approximation, almost fusion, of the paired lateral fins. From Krohn's species, however, it is easily distinguished by the absence of a constriction between body and trunk and by the numbers of the teeth and cirrhi.

The head is large, 3–4 mm. wide and 2 mm. long in a specimen 45 mm. long. It bears on each side 8–10 stout cirrhi (Greifhaken), which are strongly curved, and of which the middle three are the longest. The accessory teeth (Nebenkiefer) are arranged in two series, of which the more dorsal are 3–5 in number and are short and stout; the more ventral are 5–7 in number and are slighter and longer. The neck is somewhat thinner than the body. The body tapers without constriction to the tail; the latter (post-septal region) is less than one-fourth of the total length. The lateral fins are set rather far back, the anterior being much longer and narrower than the posterior.

The longest specimen measured 45 mm. The following dimensions are taken from well-preserved straight specimens, of which A was apparently uncontracted, B contracted considerably antero-posteriorly :—

	A.	B.
Total length	30 mm.	38 mm.
Head, „	1	2
Body, „	23	26
Tail, „	6	10
Neck, width	1·5	3
Body, width at widest .. .	2	4
Anterior fin, length	20	18
„ „ width	3	6
Posterior fin, length	10	7
„ „ width	4	9
Tail-fin, width	3	6

It is curious that this species should not have been taken by the Plankton Expedition, which records [2] *S. bipunctata* from the north of Scotland. From this it is distinguished readily by the approximation (continuity) of the lateral fins.

From *S. hexaptera* it is further distinguished by the size of the head, by the slightly more backward position of the posterior lateral fin, by the possession of more numerous cirrhi, and by the absence of the five-rayed star on the accessory teeth (*cf.* Strodtmann, *loc. cit.*).

[1] In honour of Admiral Wharton, R.N., the Hydrographer, a steady friend to oceanic research.

[2] Strodtmann, "Systematik der Chaetognathen," Arch. für Naturgeschichte, lviii. Band i. pp. 333–376, pl. xvii.

From *S. bipunctata* it is readily distinguished by the number of teeth in the accessory rows and the proportions of tail to body.

A row of stout processes is placed on the ventral side of the rows of accessory teeth. These appear to correspond to the " folliculi vestibolari " of Grassi ; but in forming a single row they differ from those which he figures as characterizing *S. hexaptera* [1].

I have been unable to detect any trace of a " corona ciliata " (Riechorgan) on the dorsal surface of the head and neck.

This species [2] appears to be present in both the " cold " and the " warm " areas [3] of the Faeroe Channel, and to be a characteristic component of the " Mesoplankton," *i. e.* the floating and swimming organisms between a depth of ±100 fathoms below the surface and a depth of ±100 fathoms from the bottom.

Horizontal distribution : 61° 18′ N., 4° 21′ W., to 59° 42′ N., 7° 7′ W.

Vertical distribution :—

Greatest depth—warm area—Sta. 19 *a*, 480 to 350 fathoms ; temp 46° to 47° F.

Greatest depth—cold area—Sta. 13 *y*, 465 to 335 fathoms ; temp. 31° to 33° F.

Least depth—Sta. 13 *i*, 100 to 0 fathoms ; temp. 48° to 54° F.

The least depth given above was the only occasion on which it was taken anywhere near the surface, except for one doubtful and broken specimen at the surface at midnight (Sta. 15). There is no doubt that this species is essentially Mesoplanktonic, with a very wide temperature range (at least 33° to 48° F.); it occurred in every haul, but one, of those made between 530 and 100 fathoms (*i. e.* in eight out of nine hauls); it occurred in every haul which began at or lower than 300 fathoms and finished at the surface (three hauls); and was taken, certainly, only once in a haul which began at 100 fathoms and ended at the surface (once out of twenty-two hauls).

SPADELLA (KROHNIA) HAMATA, Mobius.   (Plate L. fig. 4.)

Having obtained a large number of well-preserved specimens of this species, I think it worth while to give an outline (fig 4) of the external form, since both the original figure of Mobius [4] (which has been simply copied by Hertwig [5] and by Grassi [6]) and also the

---

[1] Grassi, *loc. cit. infrà*, pl. iii. fig. 6.

[2] I am anxious to leave the discussion of the bathymetric limits of the species taken on H M S. ' Research,' and of the means used to determine these limits, till the material has been more fully investigated. At the same time, in describing a new species it is necessary to provisionally indicate the depth at which it was taken, but remarks under this heading must be for the present considered as *provisional*, except in the case of surface forms

[3] For an explanation of these areas, see Wyville Thomson, ' Depths of the Sea.' London, 1874. 8vo

[4] Jahresb Commiss wissenschaft. Untersuch. deutschen Meere, Jahrg. ii., in p 158, pl iii. fig. 13

[5] " Die Chaetognathen," Jenaische Zeitschrift, xiv. pl. ix fig. 7.

[6] " I Chetognati," Fauna und Flora Golf. Neapel, v. pl. i fig. 5.

more recent figure of Strodtmann [1], owing doubtless to ill-preserved material, are capable of improvement in respect of the lateral fins. There can be no doubt that the 'Research' specimens are referable to this species, since they agree with Mobius's description and figures of the cephalic armature to the minutest detail.

This species appears to be an essentially northern form. It was originally described by Mobius from the following localities :— N. of Hanstholmen, Korsfjord (twice), and N.W. of Skagen (misprinted S.W., *loc. cit.* p. 158) during the cruise of the 'Pommerania,' 1872.

It was recorded by Levinsen [2] from Greenland (Kronprinsens Eiland), from 30 m. W. of Cape Farewell, and from lat. 59° N., long. ? ; lat. 57° 50′ N., long. 48° 43′ W.; lat. 57° 48′ N., long. 43° 45′ W.

Strodtmann records it from the North Atlantic Drift (" Gulfstream "), Irminger (Greenland) Sea, and the Labrador Current, *i. e.* from 60° to 50° N. latitude, as having failed in no single haul made by the 'National' (Plankton Expedition) in 1889.

In the Faeroe Channel it was rarely absent from a tow-net.

The deepest haul in which I obtained this species was in the warm area—Sta. 19 *a*, 480 to 350 fathoms, temperature 46° to 47° F. It may be regarded as having a fairly wide range of temperature (eurythermal), since it was obtained from the surface at a temperature of 53° F. (haul 15 *b*), and at a temperature of less than 33° F. (haul 13 *g*, 31° to 33° F.) in the cold area.

These four instances are, I believe, the only records of the occurrence of the species.

In illustration of the ease with which one may fail to collect specimens of a fairly plentiful species, may be cited two successive hauls, made within an hour of each other:

Haul 19 *a*, 480 to 350 fm., gave 6 specimens of *S. hamata*.
   ,,   19 *b*, 480 to   0   ,,   0   ,,   ,,

In other words, 6 were caught in towing through 130 fm. of water, none in towing through 480 fm. (*cf.* Strodtmann, *loc. cit.* p. 367) with the same net at the same place.

SALPA ASYMMETRICA, sp. n.   (Plate L. figs. 5–8.)

As was the case with most Salpæ collected on the 'Research,' the specimens of this species were considerably damaged by pressure against the tow-net, owing to the heavy rolling of the ship when heaved to. Not all anatomical details could therefore be satisfactorily made out, but the following appear to be good characters :—

EXTERNAL CHARACTERS —Body ovoid, flattened, devoid of processes. Apertures in *solitary form* terminal; apertures in *sexual*

[1] " Systematik der Chaetognathen," Arch. Naturgeschichte, lviii. Bd. i. pl. xvii. fig. 17.
[2] " Om nogle pelagiske Annulata," Vidensk. Selsk Skriften, (6) iii. 321.

form, mouth dorsal, cloaca terminal.   Surface smooth.   Length of sexual form 12 mm.

TEST clear, transparent, thin.

MANTLE.—In the *sexual form* the musculature exhibits an asymmetry similar to that already. described in *S. dolichosoma-virgula, musculosa-punctata*, and *magalhanica* [1].   The mouth has a pair of sphincters, apparently formed by splitting of two lateral longitudinal muscle-slips.   At least one sphincter surrounds the cloacal aperture ; but the arrangement of the musculature of both apertures was extremely difficult to make out, owing to the bad condition of the specimens.   The order, or rather the disorder, of the main muscles is more easily appreciated from drawings than from a description (Plate L. figs. 5, 6, *a–f*).   In addition to these there are two dorsal longitudinal muscle-slips, a dorsal sheet overlying the nucleus, and a fan-like sheet on the right of the nucleus.

In the *solitary form*, extracted with the placenta from the parent, the musculature is much more regular ; it consists of eight complete bands, two large and (?) four small circumcloacal sphincters (the arrangement of which could not be exactly ascertained), a right and a left longitudinal slip of unequal length in connection with the two circumoral sphincters.

ENDOSTYLE fairly long and straight.

DORSAL LAMINA large (diam. in posterior third about 5 mm. in sexual form), with strongly-marked ridges.   No languet was detected.

DORSAL TUBERCLE large, about 5 mm. in length in sexual form ; transversely marked with fine bands of cells.

VISCERAL MASS comparatively small, brownish yellow in life.

At first it seemed probable that one was dealing merely with a specimen curiously broken, and that the asymmetry was artificial. But specimens of this species were taken on many occasions, and all possibility of the above explanation was destroyed when I obtained several specimens which presented the same asymmetry, but in a "Spiegelbild," namely the reversal which would be produced by a reflection in a mirror.   The same reversal or "inverse image" has been discussed at length by Apstein [2] on the basis of the three asymmetrical genera cited above.

As the 'Ergebnisse der Plankton Expedition' are not readily accessible to everyone, and as the point is novel and of some interest, I quote Apstein's conclusions :—" Bei den übrigen Salpen, die eine symmetrische Muskulatur haben, ist Spiegelbild und Kongruenz dasselbe, bei einem unsymmetrischen Körper aber fallen Spiegelbild und Kongruenz nicht zusammen.   Ich glaube jedoch, dass bei allen Salpen in der Kette die Individuen der eine Reihe gleich, d. h. kongruent sind, aber zu denen der anderer Reihe spiegelbildlich sich verhalten, aber dass dies in der Muskulatur

---

[1] Apstein, 'Ergebnisse der Plankton Expedition: Die Thaliacea.—B. Verteilung der Salpen,' p. 17.

[2] Apstein, *loc. cit.* p. 17.

meist nicht zu sehen ist, weil fast alle Salpenarten symmetrische Muskeln haben."

This adds an eighteenth species to the list of Salpæ occurring in the North Atlantic.   It was obtained at two stations (four hauls) in small quantities   Sta. 13, 60° 2′ N., 5° 49′ W.; and Sta 19, 59° 42′ N., 7° 7′ W.   On these four hauls it was at the surface; in two more hauls at the same stations it was also taken from uncertain horizons with an open tow-net, probably at or near the surface.

EXPLANATION OF PLATE L.

Sagitta whartoni, sp. n (p. 992).

Fig. 1 Ventral view   × 2
Fig 2 Dorsal view of head, showing some of the cirrhi, the two rows of accessory teeth, and the row of sensory processes   Cam. luc × 12
Fig. 3. Cephalic armature.   a, end of cirrhus, b, tooth of ventral row, c, tooth of dorsal row.   × 210.

Spadella (Krohnia) hamata (p 993)
(Drawn by camera lucida)

Fig. 4 Ventral view   × 2

Salpa asymmetrica, sp n. (p. 994).

a–f main muscles of the mantle.
at. atriopore
cl. cloaca
dl dorsal lamina.
dt dorsal tubercle.
el. elæoblast
en endostyle
ne nerve-ganglion
nu nucleus.
pl placenta
st stolon

Fig. 5. Sexual form, dorsal aspect   × 4 5
Fig. 6 Sexual form, ventral aspect   × 4 5.
Fig. 7. Solitary form, right side   × 16.
Fig. 8 Solitary form, left side.   × 16.

2. On the Occurrence of a Pair of Supernumerary Bones in the Skull of a Lemur and on a Peculiarity in the Skull of a young Orang.   By ROBERT O CUNNINGHAM, M.D., F.L.S., F.G.S., C.M Z.S., Professor of Natural History, Queen's College, Belfast.

[Received November 9, 1896]

A short time ago, when taking part in an oral examination on zoology at the Royal University of Ireland, Dublin, I was somewhat surprised to recognize in the skull of a common Lemur a small pair of supernumerary bones intervening between the frontals, nasals, and lachrymals.   As I could not find any reference to such bones in any of the works on comparative anatomy at my disposal, I wrote to Sir William Flower, as our highest authority on the osteology of the Mammalia, to ask him if he could furnish me with any information on the point.   He kindly handed my letter with its accompanying sketch to Dr. Forsyth Major, who showed him a skull with exactly the same bones, observing that

2. Contributions to our Knowledge of the Plankton of the Faeroe Channel.—No. II.   By G. Herbert Fowler, B.A., Ph.D., Assistant Professor of Zoology, University College, London.

[Received March 29, 1897.]

The following notes form a continuation of the previous paper on this subject (see P. Z. S. 1896, p. 991):—

Conchœcia maxima (Brady & Norman).

Twenty-five specimens, apparently referable to this Ostracod, were obtained in deep-water hauls. It occurred in three hauls at depths between 480 and 220 fathoms, and in three hauls which began at depths greater than 300 fathoms and were finished at the surface; it did not occur in a single one of the twenty-two surface hauls (100 fathoms or less, to the surface).

The only other occurrences of this species are recorded by Brady and Norman[1] as " off Greenland in lat. 74° 49′ N., long. 11° 30′ W., in a depth of 350 fathoms, and by H.M.S. 'Triton' in 1882, lat. 60° 20′ N., long 7° 23′ W., in 200 fathoms, cold area, Faroe Channel."   Mr. John Murray, who supplied these specimens to Mr. Brady and Canon Norman, has kindly informed me that the Greenland specimens "were brought home by Mr. Gray in a Peterhead whaler a few years ago."

So far as the three records go, there can be little doubt that in Conchœcia maxima we have a true member of the cold Mesoplanktonic fauna.   The lowest depth and temperatures at which it was captured on the 'Research' were[2]:—

Sta. 13 g.—465 to 335 fathoms , temp. 31° to 33° Fahr.
Sta. 19 a.—480 to 350 fathoms; temp. 46° to 47° Fahr.

Tomopteris onisciformis, Eschscholtz.

Vejdovský[3] recognizes three European species of Tomopteris:— onisciformis (Eschscholtz[4]), vitrina (Vejdovský[3]), and scolopendra (Keferstein[5]).   His diagnostic characters, however, seem quite inadequate for sharp distinction, and fall in all probability within the limits of individual variation, excepting in the case of the " Flossenaugen," the remarkable structures which have been variously interpreted as eyes or as phosphorescent organs.

According to Vejdovský these are arranged as follows —

Vitrina, Vej.—One on the notopodium, one on the neuropodium; pigment yellow ; one lens.

[1] Sci. Trans. Roy. Dublin Society, (ii) v. 687, pl. lxi. figs. 1–8.
[2] Cf. Proc. Zool. Soc. 1896, p. 993 note.
[3] Zeitschrift wiss Zoologie, xxxi. p 81
[4] Isis, 1825, p. 735
[5] Arch. Anat. Physiol., 1861, p 360.

Scolopendra, Kef.—One on the neuropodium only; pigment dark red; two lenses

Onisciformis, Esch.—Two on the notopodium, two on the neuropodium; pigment yellow; five lenses.

These seem good diagnostic characters, but are unfortunately not entirely justified.

Taking first the number and position of these organs, and accepting Vejdovský's and Keferstein's account of *vitrina* and *scolopendra* respectively, the alleged presence of two "Flossenaugen" on each half of the parapodium in *onisciformis* is stated by Vejdovský to have been observed by Carpenter and Claparède [1], and by Leuckart and Pagenstecher [2]. A reference to the original memoirs shows, however, that the first-named authors describe and figure one only on the notopodium, one on the neuropodium; and that the German authors, describing a 2 mm. *onisciformis* under the name of *quadricornis,* describe and figure one only on the basal part of each parapodium. Busch [3] also, in describing young specimens, agrees with Leuckart and Pagenstecher. *Tomopteris onisciformis*, therefore, like *T. vitrina*, has apparently one "Flossenauge" on the notopodium, one on the neuropodium, or two on each parapodium; it has probably only one in young stages, and this only on certain parapodia.

Taking next the question of the pigment, its colour, yellow, dark red, or brown, can hardly be reckoned diagnostic. Lastly, with regard to the question of the lenses—these appear, according to Greef [4], who worked on fresh material at the Canary Islands, to be artificial products of the preservation fluids. Almost certainly, judged by a comparison of the figures, the five lenses attributed by Vejdovský to Leuckart and Pagenstecher's *onisciformis* are the same things as his "Augen-drüse" cells, which appear to surround the pigment-cells in a surface view.

There seems, therefore, to be no real specific distinction between Vejdovský's *vitrina* and *onisciformis* (auctt.). In my specimens of *onisciformis* the basal joint of the second cirrhi (Borstencirrhen) was sometimes longer, sometimes shorter than the first parapodium, and the eye-lenses were single—thus breaking down two more of his diagnostic criteria.

It is possible, as Vejdovský suggests, that *T. scolopendra* (Kef.) may be separate from *T. onisciformis* (?=*Briarœa scolopendra*, Quoy and Gaimard [5]); but it is always difficult, often impossible, to make certain of the "Flossenaugen" in preserved material, and conceivably *scolopendra* may prove a Mediterranean variety of *onisciformis*.

The largest 'Research' specimen measured 45·5 mm. in length;

[1] Trans Linnean Soc, xxiii p 59.
[2] Arch. Anat Physiol., 1858, p 588.
[3] Arch Anat. Physiol., 1847, p. 180
[4] Zeitschrift wiss Zoologie, xxxii p 237.
[5] Ann. Sciences naturelles, x p 235.

the second cirrhi (Borstencirrhen) were only 33 mm. long in this specimen, but in smaller ones were often longer than the body. The fully developed parapodia were 20 in number ; the undeveloped posterior part of the body carried eight rudimentary parapodia, and measured 9 mm.   In the youngest specimens the parapodia were proportionately fewer than in the medium-sized specimens, and are again less crowded in the largest.   Points like these, taken with the specific uncertainty already discussed, show how necessary is a renewed study of the genus on *living* material.

I have not found any record of a larger specimen than this, but my friend Mr. E. T. Browne informs me that he has taken a specimen about 55 mm. in length off Valentia.

As regards the horizontal distribution of the species, it is common in northern seas, but not apparently further north than the Faeroe Channel. Here it was captured by both the ‘ Knight Errant ’ and the ‘ Triton,’ and Prof M‘Intosh [1] points out that it appears to have been procured from very varying depths ; this agrees with my experience on the ‘ Research ’, it was taken at [2] Sta. 13 *g*—465 to 335 fathoms, temp. 31° to 33° Fahr., and was also taken at the surface at a temperature of 54° F.

Tracheloteuthis riisei (Steenstrup).

I have found some difficulty in the determination of this species, owing probably to the fact that Steenstrup’s original description [3] was of the briefest.

A specimen obtained in the Faeroe Channel during the cruise of H.M.S. ‘ Knight Errant ’ in 1880 was fully described by Hoyle among the ‘ Challenger ’ Cephalopoda [4], but he expressed himself as uncertain of his determination.

The deciding characteristics of the only two species [5] known appear to be the following according to Carus [6] (founded on Hoyle and Weiss) and Steenstrup :—

	riisei.	*behnii.*	‘ Research ’ spec.
Fins......	Rhomboid. C., S.	Rounded behind. C. Heart-shaped S.	Rounded behind. Heart-shaped.
	$=\frac{1}{3}$ body length. C.	$> \frac{1}{4}$ body length. C [7] $=\frac{1}{4}$ body length S.	$=\frac{1}{3}$ body length.
Tentacles	$=$body length C.	$=\frac{2}{3}$ body length. C	$=$body length.
Arm 4 ...	$=\frac{2}{3}$ length of arms 2, 3. S	$=\frac{1}{4}$ length of arms 2, 3. S.	$=\frac{2}{3}$ length of 2, 3.

While, then, the general dimensions of my specimen agree with

[1] ‘ Challenger ’ Rep. Zool., Annelida Polychæta, xii. p 532.
[2] *Cf* Proc Zool Soc 1896, p 993 note
[3] Vidensk Medd Nat. Foren. Kjobenhavn, (4) iii. p. 293
[4] Chall Rep Zool xvi Cephalopoda, pp 163–166, pl xxviii figs. 6–12
[5] Since the above was in type, I find that a third species, *T guernei*, has been described by Joubin (‘ Campagnes Scientifiques par S. A. le Prince de Monaco,’ fasc. ix), but it is not likely to be confounded with either of the other two.
[6] Prodrom Faunæ Mediterr ii pp 447, 448
[7] “ Plus quam $\frac{1}{4}$ palln æquantes ”   Surely a mistake ’

those of *T. riisei*, the shape of the fin is markedly that of *T. behnii*, this is well brought out by Hoyle's figure, which shows a distinctly rhomboid fin.

A specimen of *T. behnii* was described by Weiss [1], which agrees almost exactly with the diagnostic characters given above for that species.

The following table exhibits the dimensions of my specimens, the 'Knight Errant' specimen described by Hoyle, and the Messina specimen described by Weiss, expressed in percentages of mantle length.—

	'Research'	'Knight Errant.'	Messina.
Length of mantle in mm	23	32	21
Breadth of mantle ...	·38	·25	—
Length of fin	·34	·40	·28
Breadth of fins	·56	·59	·38
Length of arm 1	·21	24	14
„ 2	56	·56	·33
„ 3	·47	·46	·28
„ 4	·34	·40	·19
Length of tentacle....	·91	1·00	·61

So far as this goes it is fairly obvious that the 'Knight Errant' and 'Research' species are the same, and different from the Messina species; the dimensions further point to an accurate determination by Hoyle and Weiss of their respective species.

I have therefore assigned my specimen to *T. riisei*, although the shape of the tail-fin is distinctly that of the other species.

Dimensions in millimetres:—end of body to margin of mantle, 23; breadth of body, 9; length of fin, 8; breadth of conjoint fins, 13; arm i, 5; arm ii, 13; arm iii, 11; arm iv, 8; tentacle, 21.

The animal was of an absolutely glass-like transparence, except for the two staring black eyes and a black mass posteriorly (? ink-sac). When it had been killed, scattered chromatophores became more obvious, notably four, symmetrically placed on the dorsal surface of the head, and a line of smaller ones along the median dorsal line of the mantle, they were of a deep claret-colour.

As Hoyle [2] pointed out, and was corroborated by Jatta [3], *Tracheloteuthis* is a member of the subfamily *Ommastrephini*; the latter author refuses, however, to accept the suggested identification of *Tracheloteuthis* with *Verrilliola=Entomopsis*, as the four species described under these two genera are members of the *Taonoteuthi*.

Distribution:—

(1) Faeroe Channel—60° 29′ N., 8° 19′ W., surface ('Knight Errant').

(2) Faeroe Channel—60° 2′ N., 5° 49′ W., 100 to 0 fathoms ('Research').

(3) Atlantic, Mediterranean (*Steenstrup*).

[1] Quart. Journ Micr Sci xxix. pp 75-96, pls. viii.-x.
[2] *Loc. cit*
[3] Fauna e Flora Golf Neapel —I Cefalopodi (Sistematica), p 112.

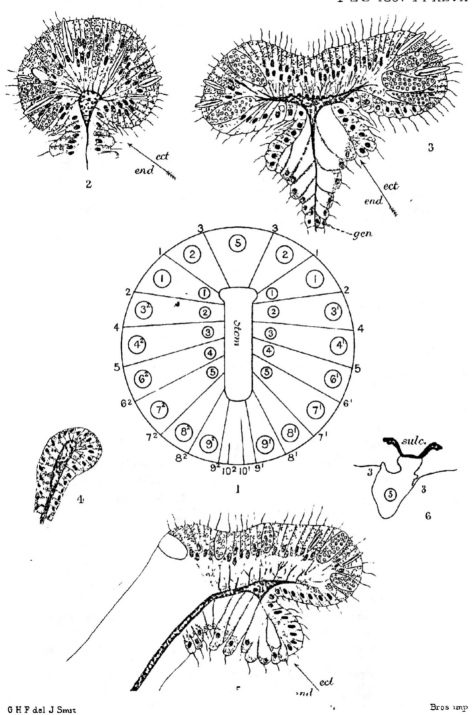

G H F del J Smit

Bros imp

HYLAMBATES JOHNSTONI, sp. n.   (Plate XLVI. fig. 4.)

Vomerine teeth in two small groups between the choanæ.   Head much broader than long; snout rounded, as long as the diameter of the eye; interorbital space as broad as the upper eyelid; tympanum two thirds the diameter of the eye.   Fingers with a slight rudiment of web; toes half-webbed; disks well developed; inner metatarsal tubercle large, compressed, crescentic, very prominent.   The tibio-tarsal articulation reaches the eye. Skin smooth above, granulate on the throat, belly, and lower surface of thighs.   Purplish or brown above, with a more or less distinct dark triangular marking on the back, the apex reaching the occiput; white dots usually scattered on the back; limbs with very indistinct dark cross-bars; a white streak borders the upper lip, the outer side of the forearm and hand, the anal region, the heel, and the outer side of the foot; hinder side of thighs dark brown; lower parts white.

From snout to vent 42 millim.

Closely allied to *H. anchietæ*, Bocage, from Angola.

Three specimens from Kondowe-Karonga, and one from the Nyika Plateau.

EXPLANATION OF PLATE XLVI.

Fig 1 *Lygosoma johnstoni*, Blgr   Side views of head and anterior portion of body and pelvic region, and upper view of head (p. 801)
    2 *Glypholycus whytii*, Blgr   Upper, lower, and side views of head (p. 802)
    3 *Arthroleptis whytii*, Blgr (p 802)
    4. *Hylambates johnstoni*, Blgr (p 803).

9. Contributions to our Knowledge of the Plankton of the Faeroe Channel.— No. III.[1] The Later Development of *Arachnactis albida* (M. Sars), with Notes on *Arachnactis bournei* (sp. n.).   By G. HERBERT FOWLER, B A., Ph.D., Assistant Professor of Zoology, University College, London.

[Received June 15, 1897]

(Plate XLVII.)

ARACHNACTIS ALBIDA (M. Sars).

This beautiful floating Actinian was originally described by Michael Sars in 1846 (*loc. cit. infrà*), it has since been taken on several occasions, and has received quite a large amount of attention.

The recorded occurrences and the references to descriptions are most simply put in tabular form.   They all refer to surface captures, often in company with shoals of *Salpæ*.

---

[1] For Part I. see P. Z. S. 1896, p 991, Part II. *antea*, p. 523.

Arachnactis albida, M. Sars.

M. Sars, Fauna littor Norveg i. p. 28	Off Floroe Island.	Autumn & winter, 1846.	Original description of the species
Forbes & Goodsir, Tr. Roy. Soc Edin. xx 307.	The Minch.	Aug 1850	Refer to Dr. Balfour having taken it in 1841.
Vogt, Archives de Biologie, viii p. 1.	56° 35′ N , 20° 19′ W.	Sept 1861.	In strong current from N E
„ „ „	Rockall to Hebrides ('Holsatia')	July 1885.	
Boveri, Zeit. wiss Zool. xlix p. 459	Faeroe Channel ('Triton')	Aug 1882.	
Vanhoffen, Bibliotheca Zoologica, IIft xx.	60° N., 7° W.	Sept. 1893	
„ „ „	? Rockall to Hebrides ('National').	1889.	German Plankton Exped.
, „ „	North Sea, near Brit coasts.	Feb to April, 1895.	? *A. bournei.*
Browne (unpublished).	Valentia Island.	⎰ Mar. 1895.	
Fowler	Faeroe Channel ('Research')	⎱ Aug 1896. July 1897.	

All recent observers of *Arachnactis* are agreed that it is to be
referred to the *Cerianthidæ*. As regards the early development of
this group, Kowalewsky[1] traced it from the gastrulation to the
formation of two pairs of tentacles and one pair of mesenteries;
but unfortunately obscured his information by writing in Russian.
Van Beneden[2], beginning where Kowalevsky left off (and giving
a short abstract of his work), traced the development of an *Arach-
actis* (apparently not *A. albida*, although described under that
name) from a stage with two pairs of tentacles and one of
mesenteries up to a stage with seven tentacles and four pairs of
mesenteries. On the later development we have also two papers:
Boveri[3] began with 8 tentacles and five pairs of mesenteries, and
carried it to a stage with 21 tentacles and 14 oral tentacles;
Vanhoffen[4] made sections of, and described in detail, a stage with
19 mesenteries.

As regards these two last papers, I am glad to say that my
observations bear out those of Boveri, but regret that they are far
from agreement with those of Vanhoffen. The latter author has
been drawn into a series of mistakes by an initial error, which is
best given in his own words :—"Die Reihenfolge in der Bildung
der Septen ergiebt sich aus der Verfolgung der Schnitte von unten
nach oben"; that is to say, he imagines that the order of development of the mesenteries can be inferred from a comparison of
their absolute length at a late stage: and it is hardly necessary to
say, not only that this assumption is quite unjustifiable, but that
the order of development which he consequently assigns to the
mesenteries proves to be absolutely erroneous when tested by
successive stages. As Vanhoffen is the latest writer on *Arachnactis*,

[1] Nachrichten d. Ges. d. Freunde d. Naturerkenntniss u s w., Moscow,
1873.
[2] Archives de Biologie, xi. p 115.   [3] *Op. cit. supra.*   [4] *Op. cit. supra.*

it seemed to me worth while to study all the stages in my power, and to endeavour to put the matter straight again.

The following stages have been drawn from 'Research' specimens and cut into microscopic sections :—

Stage	Tentacles.	Mesenteries.	Oral tentacles.
A	6	10	0
B	7	11	4

Appearance of the unpaired tentacle (5).

C	9	12	4
D	9	12	4
E	10	14	6
F	11	16	8
G	12	16	8
H	13	18	8
I	?	19	10

(First appearance of generative cells.)

A few older stages have also been studied.

This table, taken together with the diagram (Pl. XLVII. fig. 1), sufficiently shows the successive development of the various structures, and their position in the oldest specimens. As regards this diagram, the order of succession of the first four pairs of mesenteries is taken from van Beneden's account of an allied species, and that of the first two pairs of tentacles is inferred from his drawings and descriptions. The facts implied by the remainder of the diagram I have myself checked, and they will be found to differ entirely from those given by Vanhoffen, and to agree with those of Boveri on all points with which we both deal. The developmental order of the first four pairs of mesenteries, as described by van Beneden (c, a, b, d), appeared at first to contradict the lettering attached to the same mesenteries by Boveri (d, a, b, c), but the latter author courteously informs me that he did not intend by these letters to indicate a developmental succession : van Beneden's observed order may therefore be taken to hold good for this species also, in default of direct evidence.

ARACHNACTIS BOURNEI, sp. n.

' There can be no doubt that the specimens from the English Channel, first recorded by Bourne, and described by van Beneden, under the name of *Arachnactis albida*, belong to another and an unnamed species. Not only are the form and proportions of the animal quite different from those of *albida*, both in van Beneden's drawings and in a few specimens which I received from the Marine Biological Station at Plymouth in 1893, but also the rate at which different sets of organs are developed is not the same in the two species. This is at once apparent on a comparison of my table of *albida* stages (given above) with the following :—

	Tentacles.	Mesenteries	Oral tentacles.
Van Beneden's oldest larva ..	7	8	0
Plymouth specimens (1893)..	9	10	2

and while the Plymouth specimens acquire the characteristic terminal pore at a stage of between 7 and 9 tentacles, it does not become perforated in *albida* until a stage of about 8 mm. in length provided with 12 oral tentacles, or, according to Boveri, 17 marginal tentacles

Until this Channel form be traced to a known adult Cerianthid (?*C. lloydii*, Gosse), I propose to distinguish it from *A. albida* by associating with it the name of my friend Mr. G. C. Bourne, the first Director of the Plymouth Station, under the style of *Arachnactis bournei*; for although I admit that the christening of larvæ by specific names is a reprehensible practice, still so much tow-netting is now carried out every summer all round our coasts that it is advantageous that well-marked species of even larval forms should have a name under which their occurrences may be chronicled.

Arachnactis bournei, sp. n.

Bourne, J. Mar Biol Assoc (n s) i. p 321	Plymouth area	Annually [1]	Described anatomically by van Beneden, Arch Biol xi p. 115
„ „ „	Entrance to English Channel	July 1889.	
McIntosh, Ann. Mag Nat. Hist (6) v p 306	St Andrew's Bay.	June 1890	Single specimen recorded only
Vallentin, Rep R Cornwall Polyt Soc lix.	Falmouth.	Summer, 1890.	(Not seen for some years now —R. V)
Browne (unpublished)	Port Erin, Isle of Man.	Jan 1895.	
„ „ „	Valentia Island.	March 1896	

[1] According to Garstang, March and April are the chief months for *Arachnactis* at Plymouth.

From *A. albida*, which is slender and tapers markedly in late stages, *A. bournei* is recognizable by its fat cylindrical body and sharply rounded end; further, whereas in *A. albida* the union of the swollen bases of the tentacles produces an " oral disk " much greater in diameter than the body (a point better brought out by Sars' than by Vanhoffen's figure), and the tentacles are often many times the length of the body, in *A. bournei* oral disk and body have about the same diameter, and the tentacles are very short. As regards the colouring, my friend Mr. E T. Browne informs me that he has taken this form on several occasions, and that in colour it is yellowish or brownish all over : it thus presents a great contrast to *A. albida,* which is of a transparent bluish-white, except for the yellowish-brown tips of the tentacles; in older specimens of *albida* the body may also assume a brown tint, but the tentacles remain transparent even in my oldest stages. The mesenteries, in all specimens of *A. bournei* which I have been able to examine, have an extremely short course, extending only about $\frac{1}{4}$ to $\frac{1}{3}$ of the length of the body below the free end of the stomodæum; in *A. albida* they extend to $\frac{1}{2}$ or $\frac{1}{3}$ of this distance even in young specimens, and in older ones some stretch for nearly the whole body-

length. The oldest specimens of this species at present known
appear to be the Plymouth specimens with 9 tentacles.

The only other forms referable to the genus at present are
(1) *Arachnactis brachiolata*, A. Agassiz[1], obviously a different
species from either of the two already described ; (2) the larvæ
observed by Haime[2] in the cœlenteric cavity of *Cerianthus*, which
do not quite resemble either *A. albida* or *A. bournei*; with these
latter larvæ may perhaps be identical the forms discovered by
Joh. Muller and described by Busch[3] from Trieste under the name
of *Dianthea nobilis*, which have been suggested by van Beneden to
be Cerianthidan.

ORIGIN OF THE MESENTERIAL FILAMENT.

A study of the developing mesenteries of *A. albida* has confirmed
me in the belief, advocated elsewhere by myself and by others
before me on histological grounds, that the thickening at the free
edge of the mesentery, commonly known as the mesenterial filament, is ectodermal in origin. The mesenteries in *Cerianthidæ*, as
has long been known from the researches of A. von Heider[4], are
of two kinds—fertile (generative) and digestive, which generally
alternate one with another, and, as he mentions very briefly, carry
two different kinds of filaments, which become differentiated about
stage G of my specimens.

The filament of a digestive mesentery (fig. 2) is of a type familiar
to all students of Anthozoa : it consists of densely packed gland-
cells of at least two kinds, among which lie nematocysts in all
stages of development ; this tissue abuts, quite sharply and without
transition, on the undoubtedly endoderm-cells of the mesentery,
and agrees exactly in histological detail with the ectoderm of all
the stomodæum except that of the sulcus, which has small nematocysts, if any.

The filament of a fertile mesentery (fig. 3) is different from the
foregoing both in shape and in histological detail.   There is a central
groove (often deeper than in the figure) consisting of finely granular
gland-cells with very strong cilia ; these cells are practically
identical with the ectoderm of the sulcus.   The groove is flanked
by wings containing large gland-cells and nematocysts ; next to
these come three sets of simpler cells, the nuclei of the first and
third set staining very strongly.   The last of these three sets lies
"unconformably" upon the vacuolated endoderm-cells.

I venture to repeat the suggestion (due first, I believe, to von
Heider) that both types of filament are ectodermal downgrowths
from the stomodæum along the free edge of the mesentery, on the
following grounds :—

1. The histological structure of the chief part of both filaments is

---

[1] Journ. Bost Soc N. H vii p. 525 (1863)

[2] Ann. Sciences naturelles, (4) i p 341 (1854)

[3] Beob ub Anat. u. Entwickl einiger wirbellosen Seethiere, p. 122· Berlin,
1851, 4to

[4] Sitzungsber. d k.-k. Akad. Wiss. Wien, lxxix. (Math.-nat. Cl) p 204.

practically identical with that of the ectoderm of the stomodæum ; even the ectodermal pigment granules, very distinct in borax-carmine preparations on the body and stomodæum, are uniformly present on the filaments, but are not found in the undoubted endoderm.

2. Young mesenteries, which have not yet become united with the stomodæum as far down as its lower free edge, carry only a thickening of obviously endoderm-cells (fig. 4) on their free margins.

3. Mesenteries which have become united with the stomodæum as far down as its lower free edge (except the " directive " mesenteries) carry one or other of the two types of mesenterial filament above described for some distance. but below this filament they show a simple thickening of vacuolated endoderm-cells, of the same character as they carried before they reached the lower edge of the stomodæum (fig. 4); as I interpret it, the ectoderm has grown down along their free margins for some distance, but not as yet for their whole length.

4. The sulcus runs very much further down into the cœlenteron than does any other part of the stomodæum, forming a long groove of the shape indicated in fig. 6.   At the point where the ectoderm of the sulcus becomes continuous laterally with the endoderm, the histological structure is practically the same as in the filament of a fertile mesentery (fig. 5).

The only evidence, of which I know, in favour of an endodermal origin of the filament is as follows :—(1) E. B. Wilson [1], in his studies on the development of numerous Alcyonaria, claimed to have shown that the axial (dorsal) filaments were of ectodermal, the remaining six filaments of endodermal, origin. To this one may reply that Alcyonaria are not Actiniaria, although closely allied to them, and that the differentiation of function, with which Wilson showed that the different mesenteries were correlated, does not hold good in the same shape for Actiniaria. (2) The brothers Hertwig [2] refuse to accept von Heider's suggestion of an ecto-dermal origin in *Cerianthus* on the ground that in *Sagartia para-sitica* the incomplete mesenteries, which do not yet touch on the stomodæum, are provided with a filament similar to that of the complete mesenteries   This is certainly not the case in young *Arachnactis*, and, I may add, the filament of *Sagartia parasitica* seems to be in many respects of an unusual character among Actiniaria.   Neither the argument from Alcyonaria nor that from *Sagartia* appears to me to be strong enough to unseat the evidence given above. If these filaments are indeed ectodermal, the boundary between ectoderm and endoderm is obvious enough in the digestive type of mesentery ; but in the fertile type, is probably at the commencement of the vacuolated endoderm-cells, as there occurs at this point what I can only describe, by borrowing a phrase from geology, as an unconformability of strata.

[1] Mittheil. zool Stat Neapel, v. 1
[2] Die Actinien   Jena, 1879, 8vo. (Jen. Zeitschrift, xiii)

With regard to the distribution of the two types of mesenteries and filaments in *Arachnactis*, the "directive" pair practically carry no filament; for a very few sections below the end of the sulcus they have a slight thickening resembling the type of a fertile mesentery, but almost immediately assume the appearance indicated in fig 4. The mesenteries next to them are of the fertile type, and the next ensuing of the digestive type; from that point onwards the alternation is apparently regular :—

Fertile: 3, 1, 4, 6, 8, &c. } Numbered in order of
Digestive: 2, 5, 7, 9, 11, &c. } successive development.

The differentiation of the filaments of the two kinds of mesenteries in the adult *Cerianthus* is apparently not mentioned by the brothers Hertwig[1]; their figure 3, pl. viii., practically unites the main features of my figures 2 and 3. Unfortunately, the specimens of *Cerianthus* at my disposal are not very well preserved, but even in them it is obvious that there is a differentiation of the two filaments, of the same kind as, although not precisely identical with, that which I have described above for *Arachnactis*. Very young germ-cells are recognizable in both types of mesentery in the adult.

I have seen nothing in *Arachnactis* of the small "directive" mesenteries, not attached to the stomodæum, which are mentioned by von Heider as occurring in *Cerianthus*.

NOTE.—Since the MS. left my hands, I have received a letter from my friend Prof. Karl Brandt of Kiel, which informs me that Prof. van Beneden has a paper in the press dealing with the *Arachnactis* of the Plankton and other German expeditions; this will doubtless throw more light on the distribution of the various species. Prof. Brandt informs me that the genus appears to have been widely taken in the North Atlantic ('National') and in the North Sea ('Holsatia' 1885, Nordsee Expedition 1895).

EXPLANATION OF PLATE XLVII.

Arachnactis albida, M. Sars.

Fig 1. Diagram showing the order of development of mesenteries, marginal tentacles, and oral tentacles (p 805).

2 Section of the filament of a digestive mesentery, ×600 (p. 807).

3. Section of the filament of a fertile mesentery, ×600 (p 807)

4 Section of the thickened edge, presented both by a mesentery which has not touched the ectoderm at the lower edge of the stomodæum, and by a mesentery in the lowest part of its length, ×600 (p 808).

5 Section of the edge of the sulcus, ×600 (p 808)

6 Outline of the sulcus in transverse section below the level of the rest of the stomodæum, the azygos tentacle (5) and the directive mesenteries (3) are indicated also (p 808).

In Figs 2, 3, and 5, the arrow indicates the supposed junction of ectoderm and endoderm.

[1] *Op cit supra.*

November 16, 1897.

Dr. A. GUNTHER, F.R.S., Vice-President, in the Chair.

The Secretary read the following reports on the additions made to the Society's Menagerie during the months of June, July, August, September, and October, 1897 :—

The registered additions to the Society's Menagerie during the month of June were 178 in number. Of these 132 were acquired by presentation, 15 by purchase, 14 were received on deposit, 13 were bred in the Gardens, and 4 were received in exchange. The total number of departures during the same period, by death and removals, was 137.

Amongst the additions the following are worthy of notice :—

1. Two fine adult King Penguins (*Aptenodytes pennanti*), purchased out of a lot of five offered for sale by a dealer, on June 23rd.

2. A young female Orang-outang (*Simia satyrus*), brought home from Sumatra and presented by Dr. H. Dohrn, C.M.Z.S., on June 30th.

The registered additions to the Society's Menagerie during the month of July were 102 in number. Of these 34 were acquired by presentation, 17 by purchase, 14 were received on deposit, and 37 were bred in the Gardens. The total number of departures during the same period, by death and removals, was 143.

Amongst the additions attention may be specially called to :—

1. A young pair of Babirussas (*Babirussa alfurus*), from Celebes, presented by H.G. The Duke of Bedford, F.Z.S., July 3rd.

2. An example of the Thick-billed Penguin (*Eudyptes pachyrhynchus*), from Stewart Island, New Zealand, deposited by the Hon. Walter Rothschild, F.Z.S., July 5th.

3. A very large example of Daudin's Tortoise (*Testudo daudini*), deposited by the Hon. Walter Rothschild on July 21st. This Tortoise, no doubt originally from the Aldabra Islands, is said to have been kept in captivity in Mauritius for about 150 years, and is believed to be the largest Land-Tortoise now living in the world. It is about 4 ft. 7 inches in length, 2 ft. 10 inches in breadth, and weighs about 5 cwt.

The registered additions to the Society's Menagerie during the month of August were 132 in number; of these 91 were acquired by presentation, 7 by purchase, 15 were received on deposit, 18 were bred in the Gardens, and 1 was received in exchange. The total number of departures during the same period, by death and removals, was 128.

Amongst the additions attention may be specially called to.—

1. A male and two females of a large Deer from the Altai Mountains, probably referable to *Cervus eustephanus*, Blanford, received on deposit on August 10th, and apparently different in species from any Deer previously exhibited in the Society's series

3. Description d'un Genre nouveau d'Ophidiens, *Geatractus*. Par Alfred Dugès, M.D.[1]

[Received June 6, 1898]

J'ai décrit et figuré dans le Journal Mexicain 'La Naturaleza' (2ª serie, t. ii. 1897, pag. 155) un Ophidien nouveau sous le nom de *Geophis tecpanecus*.

Caractères généraux.—Aspect de Calamarien et de Coronellien. Noir à reflets bleus ; dix barres blanches dorsales, courtes et transversales ; un collier blanc passant sur la joue et la majeure partie de la gorge. Sept supralabiales, 3ème et 4ème touchant l'œil, la 5ème la plus grande. Préoculaire unique, très petite, au dessus d'une freno-oculaire. Deux postoculaires. Temporales 1+2+2 (mal rendues sur la figure) Queue extrêmement courte, robuste et obtuse. Quinze rangs d'écailles pourvues en général de deux pores apicaux. Une préanale. Tête 0 025 m., queue 0·023 m., longueur totale 0·50 m. Les vertèbres dorsales portent une hypapophyse très nette.

Mr. G. A. Boulenger a fait de ce serpent un *Atractus* (Zool. Rec. 1896, Rept. pag. 25), mais les *Atractus* n'ont pas d'hypa-

---

[1] Communicated by Mr G A Boulenger FZS

4. Contributions to our Knowledge of the Plankton of the
Faeroe Channel —No. IV.[1] Report on the Copepoda
collected by Dr. G. H. Fowler from H.M.S. 'Research'
in the Faeroe Channel in 1896 and 1897. By Isaac
C. Thompson, F L.S. (With an Appendix by Dr. Fowler.)

[Received June 18, 1898]

The material upon which this Report is based was collected in
34 out of the 41 hauls (omitting 12 f, the depth of which was not
recorded). The Plankton had been immediately preserved in
formalin, corrosive sublimate, or picric acid, and kept in 5°/₀ formalin
The Copepoda were picked out from the mass by Dr. Fowler, and
sent to me in bottles labelled with the number of the station and
letter of the haul whence the material was obtained.

By means of messengers in 1897 and of a screw-propeller in
1896 (see pp. 570–575), the mid-water tow-nets were opened and
closed at will, enabling the depths to be almost accurately ascertained, the limit of error being dependent upon the possibly impeded
rate of fall of the messenger or upon the accelerated rate of the
screw-propeller in a very heavy sea.

The accompanying distribution table records the soundings, the
depths at which the various hauls were taken, the temperature (Fah-
renheit) at those depths, the number of meshes per inch of the net
used, and the occurrences of each species. It will be seen that all
the Copepoda collected are free swimmers, with one remarkable
exception, that of *Argulus*, referred to later on.

The collection furnishes some interesting facts as to the influence
of depth upon distribution. By far the commonest Copepod in the
collection, and probably the most widely distributed species known,
Calanus finmarchicus, occurs abundantly in 32 out of the 34 hauls,

---

[1] For Part I see P Z. S 1896, p 991; Part II., P. Z S. 1897, p 523;
Part III., P.Z. S. 1897, p 803.

and appears to be equally prevalent at all depths.   But probably
no other known species exhibits this ubiquitous feature to anything
like the same extent.   A reference to the distribution table will
show that several species, such as *Heterochæta abyssalis*, were not
found at a less depth than 100 fathoms, while others, such as the
well-known and beautifully coloured *Anomalocera patersoni*, usually
remain about the surface, sometimes congregating in vast numbers.

The relative sizes of the same species at opposite depths is to a
considerable extent seen in *Calanus finmarchicus*, the deep specimens being considerably larger than those found near the surface.
Among our British Copepoda the largest known species is
Euchæta norvegica, but I am not aware that it has ever been taken
in our waters at less than 80 or 100 fathoms, at which depth I have
taken it in quantities in Loch Fyne, where it probably forms an
important item in the diet of the herring.

The vertical distribution of Copepoda is doubtless to a considerable extent subject to climatic influences.   During a continuance
of stormy weather they often altogether desert the near surface
and go very deep; while in fine warm weather many species
love to gambol on the actual surface, presenting much the appearance of the " play " of the herring in miniature.

The size of mesh in the tow-net used is of considerable importance, and the apparent scarcity of such minute forms as *Oithona
spinifrons* and *Ectinosoma atlanticum* is probably to be explained from
the fact of a large mesh having been generally used; while the
comparatively few tow-nets in which the above species were found
were of a fine texture and probably might with advantage have
been more generally employed.

Five out of seven species of Copepoda found by Dr. Brady in
material from the Faeroe Channel (Exploration of the Faeroe Channel
during the summer of 1880 in H M's hired ship ' Knight Errant '
by Staff-Commander Tizard, R N., and John Murray) occur in this
collection, viz : *Eucalanus attenuatus, Centropages typicus, Anomalocera patersoni, Acartia longiremis,* and *Oithona spinifrons*

The following species, viz., *Ætidius armatus, Euchirella pulchra,
Heterochæta abyssalis,* which occur sparingly in the collection, have
never before been recorded north of the Mediterranean, this fact
indicating a considerable extension of their distribution

CALANUS HYPERBOREUS Kroyer.

A number of what I took to be specially large specimens of
Calanus finmarchicus were found among the specimens from 20 *d*.
Careful examination clearly proves them to be identical with
C. hyperboreus, now recognized by Giesbrecht as a distinct species.
The nipple-shaped lateral terminations of the cephalothorax, the
large first abdominal segment, and the shape and position of the
teeth on the basal joint of the 5th feet appear to be the chief points
which separate *C. hyperboreus* from *C finmarchicus*.   Giesbrecht
says that joint 19 of the anterior antennæ is as long as joints 23
and 24 together; but none of the very few specimens I found with

	Station number and haul letter.	Sounding in fathoms.	Depth of haul in fathoms.	Temperature (Fahr.).	Meshes per inch of net.	Calanus finmarchicus Gunner.	Eucalanus attenuatus Dana.	Rhincalanus cornutus Dana.	Rhincalanus gigas Brady.	Pseudocalanus elongatus Boeck.	Aetidius armatus Brady.	Euchirella pulchra Lubbock.	Euchaeta barbata Brady.
Epiplankton, 0 to ± 100 fathoms.	11 a.	203	100-0	48-54	25	VA	...	...	...	...	...	...	...
	11 b.	,,	0	54	180	A	...	...	...	...	...	...	...
	11 c.	,,	30-0	49-54	36	VA	...	...	...	...	...	...	...
	12 b.	502	10-0	53	36	VA	...	...	...	...	...	...	...
	12 c.	,,	0	53	180	F	...	...	...	...	...	...	...
	12 d.	,,	150-±0	43-53	25	VA	S	...	...	...	...	...	...
	13 i.	558	100-0	48-54	36	C	F	...	...	...	F	...	...
	14 a.		0	54	180	VA	...	...	...	S	...	...	...
	15 b.	610	0	53	36	A	...	...	...	...	...	...	...
	15 d.	,,	0	53	...	A	...	...	...	...	...	...	...
	16 b.	398	0	53	36	VA	...	...	...	...	...	...	...
	16 c.	,,	4-0	53	36	A	...	...	...	...	...	...	...
	18 a.	645	3-0	53	36	VA	...	...	...	...	...	...	...
	19 c.	595	4-0	54	36	A	F	...	...	...	...	...	...
	19 d.	,,	10-0	54	36	...	...	...	...	...	...	...	...
	20 f.	560	0	52	180	...	...	...	...	...	...	...	...
	20 g.	,,	40-0	52	36	A	...	F	...	...	...	...	...
Mesoplankton, ± 100 fm. below surface to ± 100 fm. above bottom.	12 e.	502	450-320	30-32	25	A	F	F	...	...	...	F	...
	13 d.	575	400-270	32-38	25	A	C	...	...	...	...	...	...
	13 e.	,,	400-270	32-38	25	A	F	...	F	...	...	...	...
	13 g.	558	465-335	31-33	25	C	F	...	...	...	...	...	...
	16 a i.	398	350-220	31-37	25	VA	...	...	...	...	...	...	...
	16 a ii.	,,	300-170	33-44	25	A	...	...	...	...	...	...	...
	18 b.	645	530-400	31-47	25	A	...	...	...	...	...	...	...
	19 a.	595	480-350	46-47	25	C	F	...	...	...	...	S	...
	20 a.	560	200-100	39-46	40	A	...	...	...	S	F	...	...
	20 b.	,,	300-200	33-39	40	A	...	...	...	...	S	...	...
	20 c.	,,	400-300	31-33	40	A	...	...	...	...	S	...	...
	20 d.	,,	500-400	30-31	40	C	F	F	...	S	S	...	...
Doubtful depths.	12 f.	502	?10-0	?53	?36	A	C	F	...	...	...	...	...
	12 a.	,,	±350-150	±31-43	25	VA	...	...	...	...	...	...	...
	13 ab.	575	300-0	33-54	25	VA	C	C	...	...	...	...	...
	15 c.	610	530-0	30-53	25	A	...	...	S	...	...	...	...
	19 b.	595	480-0	46-54	25	O	...	...	...	...	...	...	S

Euchæta gigas Brady.	Euchæta hessii Brady.	Euchæta marina Prestandrea.	Euchæta norvegica Boeck.	Phaenna spinifera Claus.	Centropages typicus Kröyer.	Temora longicornis Müller.	Metridia longa Lubbock.	Pleuromma abdominale Lubbock.	Leuckartia flavicornis Claus.	Heterochæta spinifrons Claus.	Heterochæta abyssalis Giesbrecht.	Candace truncata Dana.	Anomalocera patersoni Templeton.	Acartia clausii Giesbrecht.	Oithona spinifrons Boeck.	Ectinosoma atlanticum Brady & Robertson.	Argulus foliaceus Linnæus.
...	...	...	...	...	...	F:	F	...	...	...	...	...	...	A	C		
...	...	...	F	...	...	F	F							A	C		
...	...	...	C	...	...	F C								A	C		
...	...	S	...	...	...	C C	C							VA	C	S	
...	...	...	...	...	...	C	C						F A	...	...	...	3
...	...	...	...	...	...	C	...						F				
...	...	...	...	...	S	...	...						S				
...	...	C	...	...	...	...	A						S F F				
...	...	S	C	...	...	...	C			C							
...	...	...	F C C C C C	...	...	...	C C C	C C F	...	...	C S					S	
S	...	C	C	...	...	...	C C	C A	S					F	S		
...	...	A	...	S	...	...	A S A	S F	...	S		S	...	F F	S		
S	S	...	F	...	...	...								F			
...	...	C	...	S	...	...	F C	...	...	...	...	S	0				
...	...	C	C	...	...	...											
...	...	A	C F	...	...	...	A C				S						
S	...	F	...	...	...	...											

perfect antennæ agree with this description. Nor, curiously enough, does Giesbrecht's own exquisitely drawn figure (pl. vi. fig. 6, Pelagischen Copepoden des Golfes von Neapel &c) bear it out.

Giesbrecht's grounds for making this a distinct species from *C. finmarchicus*, and not a mere variety, seem to me scarcely adequate. It is extremely likely that a species so widespread and living under so varied conditions should possess corresponding modifications such as we find here

The very remarkable occurrence of three specimens of *Argulus foliaceus* in 15 *d* gathering is phenomenal ; this species, so far as I am aware, having never been previously recorded except from fresh water, in which it is commonly found parasitic upon the stickleback, carp, and other fish In this instance it appears to have been taken by the tow-net as a free-swimmer ; and the only conclusion I can come to is that these three specimens became detached from a fish which had recently found its way into the sea from some stream. They in all particulars agree with *A foliaceus*, differing markedly from any of the known marine species of *Argulus*

[*Notes to Table of Distribution.*

(1) Stations 11 to 19, 1896. Station 20, 1897.
(2) The temperatures given for Station 20, hauls *a* to *d*, were not actually observed there, but are taken from the serial observations at Station 16, the difference between the two is probably trifling The serial temperatures of the 1896 cruise are published in the Report of Proceedings &c in the Faeroe Channel made by Capt. W U Moore, R N , to the Hydrographic Office in 1896
(3) For the reason of the exclusion of *Calanus hyperboreus* from the table see p 541
(4)   VA = Very abundant   C = Common.
            A = Abundant   F = Few.
                    S = Scarce

                                          G. H. F.]

Appendix to the foregoing Report. By G. HERBERT FOWLER, B A., Ph.D., Assistant Professor of Zoology in University College, London.

Mr. Thompson's Report brings out some very interesting features, from the oceanographic standpoint, with regard to the distribution and bionomics of Copepoda. The most salient feature is, as he points out, the apparent indifference of **Calanus finmarchicus** to temperature and pressure. Like *Spadella (Krohnia) hamata*, discussed for the Faeroe Channel in an earlier paper of this series[1], and on a wider basis by Steinhaus[2] and Chun[3], it is apparently equally happy whether at the surface under

[1] G H Fowler Proc. Zool. Soc 1896, p 993
[2] O. Steinhaus: Verbreitung der Chætognathen , Inaug. Dissert , Kiel, 1896 8vo.
[3] O. Chun· Beziehungen zwischen dem arktischen und antarktischen Plankton Stuttgart, 1897

pressure of 14 lbs., or at 500 fathoms under a pressure of half a ton, whether in bright light at a temperature of 54° F., or in utter darkness at a temperature of 30°–32° F.   Not only so, but it ranges apparently all over the globe (although not in such quantity [1] as in the Arctic Seas), except for the fact that it has not been recorded for the Equator and the hottest parts of the tropics, nor south of Cape Horn.   In the Antarctic regions according to Chun [2] its place is apparently taken by *Calanus propinquus*; but Mr. Thompson informs me by letter, that in a recent examination of Antarctic Plankton he finds *Calanus finmarchicus* to be one of the commonest species   Its general distribution is cited by Giesbrecht [3]

In discussing the Plankton of the Faeroe Channel it must be remembered that we are dealing with a 'Mischgebiet,' for which I would suggest the term 'Frontier,' a district in which the North-easterly continuation of the North Atlantic Drift (the so-called Gulf Stream), carrying a warm-water fauna, is constantly warring with a Southerly set of Arctic water carrying a cold-water fauna [4]. Both in 1896 and 1897 a succession of north winds had given a distinctly northern character to the fauna: and although, for example, *Ianthina*-shells and *Physophora hydrostatica* have in some cases been swept by the North Atlantic Drift as far north as the Lofoten Islands through the Faeroe Channel, I have not so far come across a single characteristically warm-water surface species in the 'Research' collections of either year from the Faeroe Channel.

Taking now the 34 hauls in which Copepoda were captured, we have 17 Epiplankton [5] hauls of less than 100 fathoms, and 13 Mesoplankton [5] hauls (including 12*a*, in which the depth was not so approximately known as in the other deep hauls, but which

---

[1] With the view of testing the Prince of Monaco's suggestion, that a tow-net could be made to provide food for shipwrecked boat's crews, we tried this species, raw, in the ward-room of the 'Research'   The Officers voted it excellent food, like "delicate shrimp-paste" '

[2] C Chun, *op cit.* p 48

[3] W. Giesbrecht Pelagische Copepoden des Golfes von Neapel, 1892, p 89

[4] Compare Chun, Beziehungen zwischen d. arktischen u. antarktischen Plankton, pp. 7–10   Stuttgart, 1897   8vo

[5] In my lectures on Oceanography at University College, I have felt the need of simple terms to express briefly the Oceanic zones, and have used the following :—

Epiplankton · 0 to ± 100 fathoms below surface

Mesoplankton · ± 100 fathoms below surface to ± 100 fathoms above bottom

Hypoplankton   ± 100 fathoms above bottom to bottom

Epibenthos. high-water mark to the mud-line (generally at ± 100 fathoms depth) = fauna of the continental shelf

Mesobenthos. the mud-line (± 100 fathoms) to ± 500 fathoms = fauna of the continental slope

Hypobenthos   over ± 500 fathoms = abyssal fauna

This is not the place in which to discuss the justification of these terms their intention will be apparent to all who have followed the recent progress of oceanic zoology. Two of them may be queried ·—(1) the Hypoplankton, under which I reckon those floating and swimming animals (Crustacea, Fish, &c.) which, for nutrition and for other reasons, are more intimately connected with

certainly finished below the 100 fathoms), in all 30 hauls, with which to deal. Regarding, then, only those species which were captured six times, or in 20 % of the hauls, as affording a sufficient basis for discussion, we find that the occurrences of seven species work out thus, expressed in percentages of hauls made above and below 100 fathoms :—

	Epiplankton.	Mesoplankton.
Calanus finmarchicus	88 2 %	100 0 %
Eucalanus attenuatus ...	17 6 „	46 1 „
Euchæta norvegica .	11 7 „	76 9 „
Metridia longa	23 5 „	69 2 „
Pleuromma abdominale	5 8 „	61 1 „
Acartia clausii	35 2 ,	15 3 „
Temora longicornis .. .	35 2 „	0 0 „

From this table it would appear (1) that *Calanus finmarchicus* is essentially eurythermal and eurybathic, *i. e.* has a wide range both of temperature and of depth ; (2) that *Eucalanus attenuatus*, *Euchæta norvegica*, *Metridia longa*, and *Pleuromma abdominale* show a distinct preference for the deep water and low temperature of the Mesoplankton, although occurring more sparingly in the Epiplankton, (3) that *Acartia clausii* belongs rather to the Epiplankton than to the Mesoplankton ; (4) that *Temora longicornis* is essentially a member of the Epiplankton. We may now compare these results, based unfortunately on but scanty data, with those recorded by others.

In the first place, **Calanus finmarchicus**, as mentioned above, has been recorded from most varied temperatures (latitudes), and is now definitely shown to extend to considerable depths (Sta. 18 *b*, 530–400 fm.). It does not occur among the Mesoplanktonic forms in Giesbrecht's list (*op. cit.* p. 788), and its vertical distribution in the Faeroe Channel is therefore worth recording It is not at present safe to suggest a maximum temperature, as expressed by mean annual isotherms, for this species ; it is, however, possible that its non-occurrence in the Equatorial region may indicate a maximum of 75° or 80° F as its temperature limit.

In the second place, it is noteworthy that of the five species of Copepoda recognized by Chun[1] as essentially Arctic types (Leit-formen), one is missing from the ' Research ' collections (*Calanus cristatus*) ; one, regarded by Mr. Thompson as a species of doubtful

---

the bottom than with the Mesoplankton , (2) the Mesobenthos, which seems on statistical and other grounds to have certain marked features, both faunistic and physical, which distinguish it from the zones below and above it , although it shares many species with other zones, still, according to the ' Challenger ' results (J Murray, Summary of Scientific Results, Exped H M S Challenger, part ii p 1430, table 1), no less than 74 per cent of its fauna is confined to it, and does not spread into other zones.

These six words, with the addition of the terms " oceanic " and " neritic " as applied respectively to the plankton of the open ocean and of the continental region, have been found in practice to serve sufficiently well for descriptive purposes.

[1] C Chun, *op cit* p 28 His list is a condensation from that of Giesbrecht, *op cit.* pp. 776–7.

value, occurred rarely (*C. hyperboreus*); one, *Pseudocalanus elongatus*, is only represented three times, and cannot therefore be further discussed; two, **Metridia longa** Lubbock (= *armata* Boeck) and **Euchæta norvegica**, are well represented. Both of these species exhibit, in the table of percentages above given, that preference for a mesoplanktonic existence which one would expect of an Arctic species in a Frontier district. For if the law be true, which was enunciated first, I think, by Moebius, that the area of distribution of a Planktonic organism is bounded at the surface by an isotherm and below by an isothermobath of the same number of degrees, we should expect Arctic forms to sink to lower (colder) depths as they approached lower latitudes (warmer surface-water). The southernmost points recorded in Giesbrecht's lists for these two species at the surface are—the northern part of the North Sea for *Euchæta norvegica*, and Concarneau for *Metridia longa* We are probably safe in assigning a maximum mean annual temperature [1] of 50° F for *Metridia longa*, and a slightly lower mean annual for *Euchæta norvegica*. In the very interesting collections made by Prof. Herdman in his traverse of the North Atlantic [2], the eight captures of *Metridia longa* were all near the mean annual isotherm of 50° F.; *Euchæta norvegica* was not captured at all. As regards the vertical distribution of *Euchæta norvegica*, the Norwegian North Atlantic Expedition failed to capture this species at the surface [3], but it certainly comes to the surface in the Faeroe Channel, even in broad daylight (Sta. 11 c).

The other two forms, which, according to the table of percentages given above, exhibit an apparent preference for the Mesoplankton—**Eucalanus attenuatus** and **Pleuromma abdominale**,—are united in having a very wide superficial range in the Atlantic and Pacific Oceans; both occur in Giesbrecht's list of mesoplanktonic Copepoda, *Eucalanus attenuatus* being credited with 1000 m = +550 fms., *Pleuromma abdominale* with 4000 m. = +2200 fms. Both these species must be regarded as eurythermal and eurybathic; and it is not at present possible to suggest a maximum or minimum temperature for either of them. Their apparent preference for the Mesoplankton in my collections must therefore be attributed to some other cause than temperature, but it is in no way inconsistent with what we already know of their habits.

Temora longicornis appears to be confined to the North Atlantic, except for two records from the Mediterranean which Giesbrecht appears to doubt [4]. So far as I am aware, it has never been recorded from any considerable depth, and with this my results accord: we may fairly regard it as a member of the Epiplankton;

[1] The mean annual temperatures are adopted from Buchan, Chall. Rep. Phys Chem. ii Atmospheric Circulation

[2] W A Herdman, I C. Thompson, and A Scott· Trans. Liverpool Biol. Soc. xii. 33.

[3] G O Sars Crustacea of the Norwegian N Atlantic Expedition, i. p. 240.

[4] W Giesbrecht, *op. cit* pp. 328–330 Mr Thompson informs me by letter that this species occurs also in a collection made at Muscat by Staff-Surgeon Bassett-Smith, R.N , of H.M.S. 'Cossack.'

and if it occurs between Newfoundland (mean annual isotherm 35° F.) and Muscat (mean annual isotherm 80° F.), it is remarkably eurythermal for an epiplanktonic animal.

As Mr. Thompson has mentioned, the occurrence of **Euchæta marina** so far north is remarkable.   It has been recorded hitherto, according to Giesbrecht and Brady, in both Atlantic and Pacific Oceans, northwards from 47° S. (?) across the tropics, but with a northern limit in the Mediterranean.   In Giesbrecht's list of mesoplanktonic species, it figures as from 4000 m. = 2200 fms. to the surface.   According to Brady[1], "it would seem to be the most abundant and most widely distributed of all the pelagic Copepoda," a description which it deserves more than ever, now that its range has been extended to the Faeroe Channel.   In Prof. Herdman's traverse it was "found in the majority of the collections taken between mid-ocean and Quebec," i. e. across the mean annual isotherms of 35° to 50° F.   Its extension northward in our longitudes is therefore by no means surprising.

The occurrence of **Euchæta barbata** and **Euchæta gigas** in the Faeroe Channel is most extraordinary.   Both species have hitherto been taken only once, and then only together, viz off Buenos Ayres (Challenger Sta. 325, 36° 44′ S., 46° 16′ W., down to 2650 fathoms). Their reappearance, still together, in northern latitudes makes it fairly safe to prophesy that the use of deep-water tow-nets in intermediate latitudes will prove them to be mesoplanktonic species of wide distribution.

Euchæta hessei (G. S. Brady), which, as Giesbrecht suggests, is perhaps identical with *Euchirella rostrata* (Claus), is known sparingly from both Atlantic and Pacific Oceans, its distribution is considerably extended by its occurrence in the 'Research' collections.

Euchirella pulchra has been recorded, according to Giesbrecht, only from the Gulf of Guinea, N W. Africa, and South America. **Phaenna spinifera, Leuckartia flavicornis,** and **Heterochæta spinifrons,** according to the same authority, are known only from the Mediterranean (including the Canaries) and from the tropical Pacific; only the last of these occurs among the species taken in Prof Herdman's traverse of the Atlantic; their range is now extended northwards to the Faeroe Channel.   They illustrate well how impossible it is at present to draw distributional areæ for most Copepoda: this group of Crustacea will probably rival the Radiolaria in the width of its distributional areæ, owing to the hardiness and tenacity of life of many of its members.   But—if we bear in mind that this is a Frontier district, i. e. one where a heavy slaughter of the Plankton occurs at the meeting of warm and cold currents, as is evinced by the abundant formation of glauconite and phosphatic nodules in the bottom deposits[2], and by the wealth of the benthos,—

[1] G S Brady, Chall Rep Zool viii. Copepoda, p 62 (*Euchæta prestandreæ*).
[2] For the glauconite, see Tizard and Murray, Proc Roy. Soc Edinburgh, i. pp 671 *et seqq* —"There were no very large phosphate nodules, but numerous small ones, with phosphates in varying quantities," in a letter from Sir John **Murray**

it is not a little suggestive that the above four species (to which may perhaps be added *Euchæta hessii* and *Candace truncata*), which appear to have wandered north of their usual habitat, were only taken in the 'Research' from the Mesoplankton, and in all cases marked by Mr. Thompson as "Scarce." All six occurred once only, except *Euchæta marina*, which was captured twice. It seems at any rate possible that these wanderers had either been killed by a reduced temperature, or at any rate so numbed by cold as to be gradually sinking to the bottom

Acartia clausii of Giesbrecht has been separated by that author from *A (Dias) longiremis* ot Lilljeborg, he uses the latter specific name for species from the Baltic and Sound only Assuming his view to be correct, the area of *A. clausii* has been somewhat extended northwards by the 'Research' collections: it reaches southwards to the Canary Islands, including the Mediterranean I gather, however, from Mr. Thompson that he himself would prefer to regard the Baltic and North Atlantic forms as varieties of one species.

A. clausii appears to have been known hitherto as an epiplanktonic form only [1]. Possibly its occurrence in deep water, at Station 20, may be due to dead or numbed specimens sinking from the surface ; but it was so regular in its appearance on that occasion (in three out of four mesoplankton hauls), that, it the above explanation be correct, a very large swarm of this species must have succumbed to cold recently As it did not occur in my mesoplankton hauls in 1896, I should prefer to leave the question open.

Rhincalanus cornutus and **Aetidius armatus** have been sparingly recorded from both Atlantic and Pacific Oceans, but not, so far as I know, from as far north as the Faeroe Channel.

As regards the remaining species in Mr. Thompson's list, there does not appear to be anything of mark connected with their appearance in the 'Research' collections, with the exception of *Argulus* (cf p. 544).

The following conclusions as to vertical distribution appear to be justifiable on a comparison of the 'Research' collections with other records :—

Calanus finmarchicus is eurythermal and eurybathic.

Metridia armata and *Euchæta norvegica*, two essentially Arctic types, tend to descend to the Mesoplankton on reaching lower latitudes

Eucalanus attenuatus and *Pleuromma abdominale* are apparently eurythermal and eurybathic.

Temora longicornis and *Anomalocera patersoni* are apparently confined to the Epiplankton.

[1] F. Dahl, Verhandl deutschen zool Gesellsch 1894, p 64.

5. Contributions to our Knowledge of the Plankton of the Faeroe Channel.—No. V.[1] Report on a Collection of very young Fishes obtained by Dr. G. H. Fowler in the Faeroe Channel. By ERNEST W. L. HOLT.

[Received June 18, 1898]

(Plates XLVI. & XLVII.   )

My friend Dr. G. H Fowler has asked me to name, if possible, the fishes taken in his vertical self-closing tow-net in the Faeroe Channel. My task is rendered the easier by the fact that the greater number of them prove to belong to one species. Individually some of the stages represented could hardly be definitely identified, even generically, but the series is practically complete and has enabled me to add considerably, as I venture to suppose, to our knowledge of the developmental phases of deep-sea forms. Incidentally the species in question, *Scopelus glacialis*, is definitely added to the British fauna, though that is a matter of no great importance. In the case of a pelagic egg and some early larvæ of very elongate form, I have only been able to point out the possible affinities. Two other larvæ, those of *Sebastes norvegicus* and *Gadus æglefinus*, have already received attention at the hands of other observers, but the collection furnishes a stage of *G. æglefinus* that has not hitherto been adequately described. The importance of a really efficient self-closing net, even from the point of view of the mere ichthyologist, can hardly be overrated.

SEBASTES NORVEGICUS Ascan. Norway Haddock.

Sebastes marinus, Collett, Norw N. Atlant. Exped., Fish. 1880, p. 15, pl. 1. figs. 3, 4.

Collett refers to this species a number of larvæ or fry which were taken at the surface "in mid-ocean, some nearly 400 kilom. from land," off Beeren Island and Spitzbergen. His examples measured from 9·5 to 19 mm , and two, illustrating the extreme terms of the series, are figured   In the brief description appended the character of the interorbital space and other obvious points of distinction from *Scorpæna dactyloptera* are not mentioned ; but we are not entitled to suppose that so careful an observer would have overlooked the possibility of confusion between the two forms.

Dr. Fowler's specimen, 12 5 mm. in length (inclusive), corresponds so closely to Collett's figures (allowing for the difference in dimensions) that it is unnecessary to illustrate it. It appears to be nearly identical in development with a North Atlantic specimen of 12 mm., but the bony ridge of the nape terminates in a single instead of in a double spine. The interorbital space is, in the Faeroe Channel larva, very wide and flat, a character in which

[1] For Part I see P Z S 1896, p 991 , Part II , 1897, p. 523 , Part III., 1897, p 803; Part IV., *antea*, p. 540.

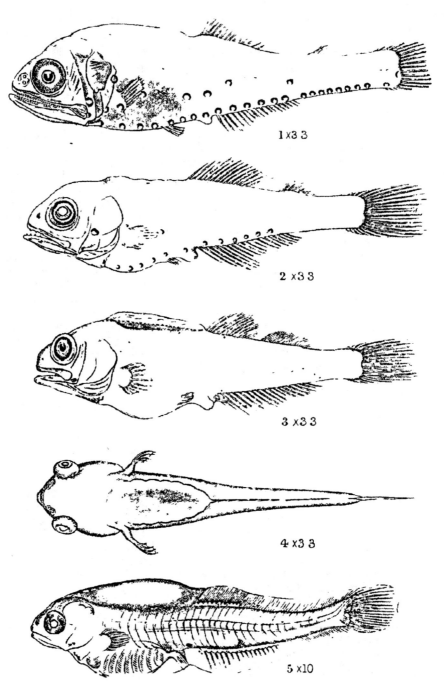

1 x3 3

2 x33

3 x33

4 x3 3

5 x10

EWLH del PJ Smt ith

Mirtern Bros imp

PLANKTON OF THE FAEROE CHANNEL

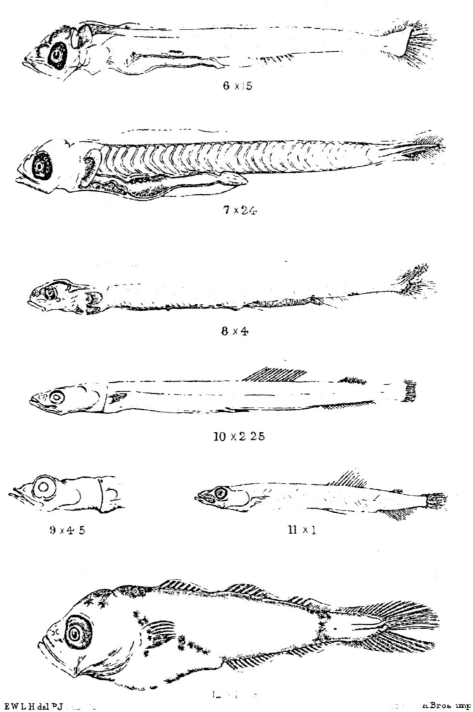

6 x 15

7 x 24

8 x 4

10 x 2 25

9 x 4 5

11 x 1

E W L H del PJ n Bros imp

PLANKTON OF THE FAEROE CHANNEL

the adult *S. norvegicus* differs most strikingly from *S. dactyloptera*. I infer, from the condition of young examples of 40 mm., that the approximation of the eyes manifests itself, in the last-named species, at a very early stage.

The specimen occurred at 60° 2′ N., 5° 49′ W., 100 to 0 fath Fragments of a little fish, taken at 60° 16′ N., 5° 49′ W., 200 to 100 fath., seem to have belonged to a member of this species, about 20 mm. long.

Collett records examples of 62 to 143 mm. from the bottom at 120 to 150 fathoms. If I have correctly identified Dr. Fowler's larger specimen, it would appear that the younger stage occurs in mid-water as well as at the surface.

GADUS ÆGLEFINUS Linn.   Haddock   (Plate XLVII. fig. 12.)

Gadus æglefinus, G. O. Sars, Rep. Cod Fish. Lofod. (1866, 1867), in Comm. Rep. U.S Comm. Fish Fisher (1877), 1879, p. 590; McIntosh, 15th Rep. Fish Bd Scot. 1897, p. 196, pl. v.

The collection contains only one Gadoid, viz a Gadus measuring 8 mm. without the caudal rays and terminal process of the urochord. It is in a good state of preservation, and may be identified with approximate certainty as a young Haddock. The eggs and very early larvæ of this fish are well known [1], and later stages, from 19 mm. upwards, have been well figured by McIntosh. Intermediate conditions have received less attention. Such were known to G. O. Sars, who probably studied them exactly; but, in the only account which I have seen, the Norwegian observer simply remarks that they are distinguishable from corresponding stages of the Cod, *G. morrhua*, by their shorter and stouter shape. McIntosh describes very briefly some specimens of 7 to 8, 11, 12·5 and 19 mm , which he attributes to the Haddock. He supposes that the smaller of the series correspond to the stages taken by Sars.

My figure (Plate XLVII. fig. 12) shows what I suppose to be the essential features of the Faeroe Channel specimen. The proportions and conformation being accurately drawn, need no elaborate description. As in the case of the young Haddock studied by Sars, the form is much more massive than in the Cod. This is seen at once on comparing my drawing with Prince's figure of a Cod, ·33 in., 8 25 mm. *a*. The total length is about the same, but the larval Cod is much more slender and appears less advanced in general development. The eye is also smaller. Probably whatever postmortem shrinkage may have occurred in one specimen is compensated by a similar condition in the other, and even if the Cod were drawn from a living specimen the difference in conformation is too striking to be entirely explained by a possible distortion of the supposed Haddock. In the latter the pelvic fins are indicated, if at all, by a very slight prominence of the thoracic region. The dorsal and anal fins are indicated by the inflections of the embryonic fin, but only a few of the permanent fin-rays are

[1] *Vide* McIntosh and Prince. Trans. R. S. Edin., xxxv. 1890, p. 822

in visible process of development. The caudal fin shows features of interest. The extremity of the notochord forms the axis of a lanceolate mass; its extremity is bent up at an obtuse angle, and a considerable part projects freely, being succeeded, to the margin of the fin, by fine embryonic rays. Dorsally occur 12 rays, or 11 and a mass of embryonic rays dividing the last true ray from the urochord. None of these show any distinct basal element. Below the urochord is a roughly trigonal hypural lobe bearing five rays. Anteriorly are three smaller oblong lobes, the most posterior bearing two, the others one ray each. In front occur 6 rays. None of these caudal rays are perfectly formed, the anterior rays, dorsally and ventrally, being but little different from the embryonic rays in front of them. The notochord is still imperfectly segmented, and the myomeres cannot be counted with accuracy. These characters, therefore, like the fin-ray formula, are not available as aids to specific determination. Preserved in formol the specimen naturally possesses no yellow pigment, if any ever were present. The black chromatophores have the distribution shown in my figure on the left side. On the right side there are in addition a few scattered chromatophores. The roof of the peritoneum is seen to be densely black when the specimen is clarified. McIntosh makes no mention of the caudal pigment-bar which is such a prominent feature in the Faeroe Channel Gadus. The chromatophores above the insertion of the pectoral in the latter probably correspond to " a very distinct area of pigment-points behind the pectorals " in Scottish larvæ of 11 mm., and ultimately perhaps to the more posteriorly situate spot of the adult. The development of pigment in Teleostean larvæ is undoubtedly influenced to some extent by conditions of light and, apart from this, is variable in individuals. Probably such differences of coloration as may exist between the Faeroe Channel specimen and those attributed to the Haddock by Professor McIntosh are explicable in this way, but the information afforded, both as to pigment and conformation, in the case of the latter only permits of a conjecture as to their identity. The Scottish examples of 24 mm. and upwards, which are figured and adequately described, are undoubtedly Haddock, and appear to be certainly derivable from such a stage as is exemplified in the larva from the Faeroe Channel

Dr. Fowler's specimen was taken at 60° 2' N., 5° 49' W , at 100 to 0 fathoms   I have myself recorded the capture of spawning Haddock at 154 fath., off the W. coast of Ireland, while Grimsby line-fishermen have told me that they frequently take the species at depths of more than 100 fath on the wide area which they include in the Faeroe Bank.

SCOPELUS GLACIALIS Reinh. (Plate XLVI. figs. 1–5 ; XLVII. figs 6, 7.)

S. glacialis, Gunther, Chall. Rep., Zool. xxii., Deep-Sea Fishes, p. 196; Lutken, Spol. Atlant., Scopel. 1892, p. 30 (250).

Myctophum glaciale, Smitt, Hist. Scand. Fish. ed. 2, ii. p. 941.

? *S. scoticus*, Gunther, Chall. Rep., Zool. xxxi., Pelagic Fishes, p. 31.

S. mulleri, Collett, Norweg. N. Atlant. Exped., Zool., Fish. p. 158

Benthosema mulleri, Goode & Bean, Ocean. Ichth p. 76.

Young, imperfectly characterized stages of the *Scopelidæ* have been a source of much labour to the various observers who have had occasion to name collections of this group, since it has been quite impossible to determine, in the absence of sufficient material, whether certain differences have a systematic or merely a developmental value. I think I am right in saying that the reproduction is quite unknown, and I can find no description of the early larvæ of any species. With regard to one, the efficiency of Dr. Fowler's vertical net appears to have supplied this want, as I find in his collection what appears to be a nearly complete series of *Scopelus glacialis*.

Though the method has its disadvantages, it appears necessary in the present instance to describe the different stages in the inverse order, commencing with the most advanced. This is a specimen of 58·5 mm., exclusive of the lower jaw and the caudal fin-rays[1]. It has the adult characters peculiar to the species and, except that most of the scales have gone and some of the fin-rays are broken, is in good preservation. No description is necessary except for ontogenetic comparison. The radial formula is D. 13, A 18. The eye is nearly three times as long as the snout, and is $\frac{5}{12}$ of the length of the head (12 mm.), which is equal to the height of the body at the shoulder and a little more than $\frac{1}{5}$ of the total length. The anal commences nearly opposite the middle of the dorsal. Adequate figures of the adult stage, which is practically exemplified in this specimen, are given by Goode and Bean and by Smitt, but in some copies of the Hist. Scand. Fishes the printing is very imperfect. A clear diagram of the photophores is given by Lutken.

Figures 1 to 7 (Plates XLVI & XLVII) represent younger stages in Dr. Fowler's collection The most advanced of these, fig. 1, measures only 14·5 mm., and has no scales; but the condition of another specimen indicates that the body is covered under natural conditions with dark-coloured scales. The part shaded in my drawing remains, in formol, a bluish grey. The photophores, having the formula of *S. glacialis*, are intact The radial formula is D 12 or 13, A. 18. The proportions of the head, eye, and snout are respectively as 31 (= 4 mm.), 10, 7. The eye is thus much smaller, relatively, than in the specimen of 58·5 mm., and the snout longer. Considered in the light of the ordinary ontogenetic changes of these parts in Teleosteans, this condition would appear to prove that the two individuals belong to different species, since as a general rule the eye decreases and the snout increases as development advances. In *Scopelus*, as I shall show, this condition is reversed during some part of the metamorphosis of the larva.

---

[1] This limitation is implied in all measurements of total length in this paper.

A specimen of 13·5 mm. does not differ greatly from the last. It was evidently fully clad, in life, with dark-coloured scales. The radial formula is D. 11 or 12, A. 15 or 16. I can see no certain indication that any rays have been entirely lost.

A specimen of 12 mm. (fig. 2) has the radial formula D. 14 *ca*., A. 18. There are no signs of scales. The photophores are incomplete, but such as are present correspond in position to those of fig. 1 and of *S. glacialis*. A low wrinkled ridge of skin occurs along the back from the nape to the first dorsal fin. The proportions of the head, eye, and snout are as 25 (=3·5 mm.), 7, 6. There is thus a further reduction in the eye and increase in the snout as compared with the 14·5 mm stage; but I think it will be conceded that the two specimens (figs. 1 and 2) are specifically identical. A vertical from the commencement of the anal passes a little behind the front of the dorsal. The base of the adipose is more extended than in the last stage.

Fig 3 shows a specimen of 11·5 mm. The radial formula is D. 14 *ca*., A. 18 *ca*., the rays being rather indistinct in the posterior parts of the fin. The adipose is continued forward by a fold of membrane, beset with numerous embryonic rays, reaching nearly to the base of the dorsal, but its permanent region is indicated by an interneural prominence of the dorsal contour. The proportions of head, eye, and snout are as 25 (=3 mm.), 7, 6, a further reduction of the eye being thus indicated. The specimen is drawn in a rather oblique position. Viewed in exact profile, the top of the eye does not quite reach the cephalic contour. No photophores appear to be fully developed, but one is indicated at the lower extremity of the preoperculum, while some pigment on the mandibles seems to be representative of others. A patch of pigment occurs on the isthmus. Except in the eyes no other external pigment is visible; but internally a black mass in the postero-dorsal part of the abdominal cavity, visible when the specimen is clarified, is probably associated with the air-bladder. The greater part of the abdominal cavity is occupied by a voluminous intestinal tract beset with transverse ridges. The liver is comparatively small, and occurs below the basal part of the pectorals. Posterior to this line the whole cavity, so far as I can see, is occupied by the intestine, which passes by a slight constriction into the pyriform rectum. The mouth is smaller than in the more advanced stages, a condition familiar in the ontogeny of the Salmon

The most remarkable feature of the larva is a large bladder-like expansion of the skin of the dorsum between the head and the dorsal fin. In the present condition of the specimen it is somewhat collapsed and flattened, its edges projecting from the upper part of the sides. Figs. 3 and 4 show this structure from different points of view, the true dorsal contour being indicated in the profile drawing by a dotted line. It is obviously identical with the wrinkled fold already noted in the 12 mm. stage, which is the degeneration of what is evidently a larval organ. In the specimen of 11·5 mm., the cavity contains an amorphous plasma, which disappears in a clarifying medium.   The larvæ of many Teleosteans, e. g., *Gadus, Solea*, are characterized in the vitelligerous condition by an expansion of the anterior part of the dorsal marginal fin, the walls of which are separated and form a sinus of varying size filled by a transparent fluid[1].   The fluid being lighter than the body and yolk, enables the larva to maintain a vertical position, as I have been able to note by watching larvæ of *Gadus luscus*, in which the sinus is well developed.   Larvæ not furnished with such a sinus in the vitelligerous stage are seldom vertical in position when at rest, except in the case of large vigorous forms from demersal ova, in which the organs of locomotion are far advanced at the time of hatching.   I regard the structure noted in our *Scopelus* larvæ as homologous with the sinus of early Gadoid and other larvæ.   It may be, as Ryder supposes, a lymph-space, having nothing in common except contiguity and continuity with the embryonic fin-fold, but I think its function is primarily connected with equilibrium.   The most remarkable feature is its persistence, in *Scopelus*, to a comparatively advanced stage of the general development.   In *Gadus* &c it appears after hatching and attains its greatest development at about the end of the vitelligerous period or a little after (as in *G. morrhua, teste* Ryder), but disappears, so far as my experience goes, before the permanent median fins commence to appear.

[(*Note added Aug.* 1898.) My friend and teacher, Professor Howes, has called my attention to the possibility of an homology between the dorsal sinus of the young *Scopelus* and a peculiar pad-like process at the anterior end of the dorsal marginal fin of the larva of *Rana alticola*, described by Mr. Boulenger in his Catalogue of the Batrachia.   Through the kindness of the last-named observer, I have been able to examine a larva of *R. alticola*.   In both cases the structures are continuous with the walls of the marginal fin, but they appear, at present, to have little else in common.   In *Rana* the median pad is associated with paired organs of a similar nature, and all three are solid and (*teste* Boulenger) glandular.   In *Scopelus* the thin-walled sinus is probably devoid of well-developed glandular matter, but the material is too valuable to be submitted to the arbitry of the microtome.

Although Dr Fowler's youngest examples of *Scopelus* are too much injured to admit of an exact determination of the extent of the sinus, it appears probable that the latter covers an area sufficiently extended to include the sites of all the glandular pads of *R. alticola*.   It is possible that the sinus is an organ of extreme antiquity, of which the isolated pads of *Rana* may be modern derivatives.]

In a specimen of about the same stage of development as that

---

[1] *Vide* Ryder, Rep Comm. Fish U S. A for 1885 (1887), p. 496, pl. 1. This author does not regard the sinus as part of the larval fin-fold, though its walls are continuous with that of the latter.

last described, the dorsal sinus is collapsed and flattened from side to side, having therefore the appearance of a skinny median ridge. A similar condition appears to have almost certainly furnished the most striking feature of Vaillant's genus *Anomalopterus* (Exp. Sci. Travaill. Talism., p. 160, pl. ix.), which is founded on a specimen of 60 mm. having a kind of adipose fold (" repli, sorte d'adipeuse") occupying the entire length of the back from the head to the dorsal fin. Presuming in an allied family such a developmental increase in the size of the eye as we have seen to occur in *Scopelus*, it appears to me quite possible that *Anomalopterus pinguis* is only a young stage of *Bathytroctes*, the dorsal fold being merely a larval sinus [1].

A younger stage of *Scopelus* is represented in the Faeroe collection by a larva of 8 mm. (as slightly bent), shown in fig. 5. The general conformation appears to clearly associate it with the stage last described. The proportions of head, eye, and snout appear to be as 15, 4, 3, but the posterior boundary of the head is ill-defined and may be farther back than is indicated by my measurements. Relatively to the snout the eye is certainly a little larger than in the last stage There is a continuous marginal fold, ampullated in the anterior dorsal region, the walls of the sinus extending some little way on to the sides. The dorsal is represented by a prominent interspinous ridge, beset with embryonic rays, but destitute of definite permanent rays. The rest of the dorsal fold bears embryonic rays, the adipose being merely indicated by a prominence of the dorsal contour. Comparing the various stages observed, it would seem that the development of the adipose proceeds on the same lines as the first dorsal and anal, since in the 12 mm stage (fig. 2) there is an indication of the formation of true rays, which, however, is never consummated. The caudal is in an advanced stage of the familiar metamorphosis, the tip of the urochord projecting very slightly. The anal, more developed than the dorsal, already shows the proximal parts of 16 true rays. Thickened processes of the body-wall external to the origin of the rectum probably represent the developing pelvic fins. The alimentary viscera appear to be in much the same condition as at 11 mm. The anterior part of the abdominal tract is masked by the base of the pectoral and the liver. The rest of the cavity is occupied by a voluminous intestine lined with well-marked annular or spiral ridges. There is little or no black pigment in the peritoneal roof. Externally black pigment is distributed as shown in fig 5. An aggregation near the lower end of the preopercular ridge and another above the middle of the anal fin appear to represent photophores, though no supra-anal photophore is indicated in the more advanced stage of 11 mm. There are about 33 myomeres, of which about 11 or 12

[1] In Vaillant's plate (*loc cit*) is a figure of *B. melanocephalus* above that of *A pinguis* Allowing for developmental changes on the lines indicated above the two are much alike, but the radial formulæ given in the text are not quite in harmony.

are abdominal. The posterior region of the tail is imperfectly segmented

Two less advanced larvæ, 6 5 and 4·5 mm. in length, may be taken together. The smallest, fig. 7, has about 31 myomeres, some 14 overlying the alimentary tract. The tail is practically diphyceical The specimen of 6 5 mm, fig. 6, has the caudal metamorphosis more advanced, and shows an early condition in the development of the anal fin. The alimentary canal is much alike in both, but in the smaller the anterior part is nearly straight. In the larger there is a slight post-œsophageal dilatation, presumably the stomach. This is followed by a (pyloric?) constriction, distal to which the gut at once expands and is slightly bent towards the left side in front. Posteriorly it tapers to the region of the rectal valve. I cannot detect distinct transverse ridges, but there are some indications of a folding of the lining membrane of the wider anterior part, and I think that this condition may well represent an earlier stage of the voluminous intestinal tract of the more advanced larvæ A large stellate chromatophore in the abdominal roof, about midway between the supposed pylorus and the anus, apparently overlies a small vesicle, not very clearly outlined This may represent the air-bladder, and there are indications of its connection by a duct with the anterior part of the alimentary canal. In both specimens the marginal fin-fold is much abraded, but is certainly ampullate in its anterior region I have not attempted in my drawings to restore it to what may be presumed to be the natural proportions. The teeth are small and not very numerous. The proportions of the head, rather injured in both specimens, are, I think, correctly represented in the drawing[1].

The general conformation, proportions of abdomen, and a sufficient harmony in the number of myomeres seem to reasonably connect these larvæ with the smallest (8 mm.) of the series of *Scopelus glacialis*[2]. It may be objected that in the undoubted *Scopeli* of 11 mm. and upwards, the proportions of snout and eye have been shown to change in a manner inverse to that which obtains in the two smallest larvæ. I think, however, the increase of the eye is a secondary condition of comparatively recent establishment. In the earliest stages I imagine that the eye and snout retain the proportional metamorphosis common in the development of Teleosteans, the snout gradually elongating as development proceeds. This would go on until the attainment of a condition roughly corresponding to that shown in fig 5. Thereafter the eye commences to increase in size until the adult proportions are attained. Such a condition appears to me more natural than an entire inversal of the metamorphosis whereby the ordinary proportional growth of eye and snout would be reversed from the earliest stage of larval development. In *Arnoglossus laterna* the

[1] The specimen of 6 5 mm has only one eye, which, whether naturally or otherwise, is oblique in position
[2] For an intermediate specimen, see note on p 560

eye of the male is known to enlarge as a secondary sexual
character associated with the development of other structural
changes; while according to Grassi[1] the Common Eel (*Anguilla
vulgaris*) acquires large eyes in deep water and in the Roman
cloacæ. The secondary enlargement of the eye in *Scopelus* is
thus not without parallels. *Scopelus* is, I suppose, a form driven
from littoral regions to a pelagic and bathybial mode of life,
involving an enlargement of the visual apparatus

Among the pelagic fishes enumerated by Gunther in his
'Challenger' monograph (vol. xxxi.) are mentioned a number of
small *Scopeli* taken by the 'Triton' in the Faeroe Channel (*loc. cit.*
p. 31). While recognizing the close resemblance which these
forms bear to *S. glacialis*, the author considers that certain
characters deserve specific distinction, and has accordingly described them under the name of *S. scoticus*.

The largest specimen measures 14 5 mm., that is, exactly the
same as the *S. glacialis* shown in figure 1. In the dimensions of
the eye (naturally considered by Gunther, in the absence of any
information of the developmental changes of this organ, of
importance) the two forms are in practical agreement. The
contour of the snout appears to agree with the corresponding
stages in Dr. Fowler's collection. The posterior margin of the
preoperculum is described as vertical in *S scoticus*, it is rather
oblique in *S. glacialis*. In the characters of the maxilla the two
forms agree. The photophore formula is described as identical
with that of *S. glacialis*. In *S. scoticus* the origin of the dorsal is
nearer to the root of the caudal than to the tip of the snout, and
is behind that of the pelvics. In *S glacialis* of 14·5 mm. the dorsal
arises midway between the snout and the caudal, in a specimen of
11 mm. it is a little nearer to the latter; and comparison of the
several young stages suggests that in relation to the two points
named there is during development a slight variety in the position
and perhaps a developmental migration of the fin. It is behind
the base of the pelvics even in adults. Younger stages do not
differ in any important detail described from those in Dr. Fowler's
collection, but specimens of 9 mm. are stated to have the fin-rays
perfectly differentiated. In this case the length given appears
from the context to include the caudal fin. One specimen of 8 mm.
(without caudal) has the rays of the dorsal still undifferentiated.
Individual variation in the degree of development at a given size
is, however, a common feature in Teleostean ontogeny. The
radial formula of *S scoticus* is stated as D. 10/11, A. 16. That of
S. glacialis is, according to Goode and Bean, D. 12–14, A. 16–18.
In Dr Fowler's specimens the formula, as we have seen, is D. 12
or 13 to 14 (?), A. 18 and 18 *ca.*, with the exception of one which
has only D. 11 or 12, A. 15 or 16. This last specimen is one of
the most advanced, in good preservation, and of nearly the same
size as another, from which it differs in no detail except the
number of fin-rays. I believe that all Dr. Fowler's *Scopeli* can

[1] Q J. M. S xxxix. 1896, p 385

safely be assigned to *S. glacialis,* and am strongly inclined to
consider that *S. scoticus* must be relegated to the synonymy of that
species.

In all 15 specimens were obtained on the ' Research '

Sta	Depth in fathoms	Temp. Fahr	Spec.	Length in mm
13 b.	300–170	° °	1	14 5 ca
13 e [1]	400–270	32–38	{ 2	6 0, 6 5 ca
			3	11 0 to 14 ca
13 g.	465–335	31–33	1	14 0 ca
13 i.	100–0	48–54	3	4 5, 7 5, 8 0.
15 c.	50–30	30–53	1	58 5
16 a.	350–170	31–44	{ 2	12 ca
			1	larger injured.
19 a	480–350	46–47	1	14 5
20 c	400–300	31–33	1	13 5

[1] 13 e is suspected of having closed nearer to the surface than the depth here
recorded; till all its contents have been identified, it is to be regarded as
doubtful —G. H. F

Many of these specimens have been more or less injured, but
all can be clearly associated with the series which I have described.
Gunther, Collett, and Goode and Bean agree in regarding *S. glacialis* as a truly bathybial species; but Dr. Fowler's self-closing net
furnishes us with the first certain evidence of its vertical
distribution   It extends evidently to at least 350 fath., the
specimen taken at 480 to 350 fath. being one of the most
advanced of the series (fig. 1)   This latter specimen enables us
to add *S. glacialis* to the British list, the locality lying within
Norman's British Area (Ann. Mag. Nat. Hist. 1890, v. p. 345).
All the other specimens occurred just outside this area as did also
the ' Triton' specimens (*S scoticus*); the latter were taken in the
Faeroe Channel " partly with a surface-net at night, partly with
the tow-net, which with a line of 350 and 600 fathoms was
worked at various depths" in the Cold Area.

S. glacialis is known from the Northern coasts of Norway,
coast of Greenland, Arctic Ocean, and various localities in the
American North Atlantic

[With regard to the vertical distribution of this species,—in the
first place, it appears to be essentially a cold-water form.   Collett [1]
records it as having been taken by the ' Voringen' once " found
floating," and once (three specimens) from 1110 fathoms west of
Hammerfest.   Previously to this expedition it had been known
only from Greenland and Northern Norway.   It has since been
taken by the ' Blake' [2], at considerable depths only, off the coasts of
New England and South Carolina, in the cold undertow which
passes under the Gulf Stream and whose upper edge forms the
Labrador current and its continuation southward.

[1] Norweg North Atlantic Exped, Fishes, p 112
[2] Goode & Bean Bull Mus Comp. Zool Harvard, x p. 222 (1883)

Secondly, like many other cold-water forms, it appears to be eurybathic in high latitudes, the difference in temperature between the superficial and deeper water being comparatively small, and offering no marked thermal barrier to its descent

Lastly, as regards the Faeroe Channel, it is noticeable that no specimens, larval or adult, were taken at the actual surface in twenty-five hauls; that the smallest specimen of all was captured nearest to the surface, between 100-0 fathoms (Sta. 13 z.); that other larvæ were taken in six out of the thirteen deep hauls, and may thus fairly be ranked among Mesoplankton. One (?) adult specimen was taken in a haul which began at 530 fathoms and finished at the surface; this unfortunately gives us no help. Although none of the 'Research' specimens were captured at the surface, still if, as Mr. Holt suggests, Dr. Gunther's *Scopelus scoticus* is identical with these larvæ, some larvæ come to the surface at night in the Faeroe Channel.

Though more observations are required for confirmation, still it seems probable that *Scopelus glacialis*, at any rate as regards the Faeroe Channel, falls into the category of animals which have an early epiplanktonic stage, but frequent greater depths when adult (*cf* p 578, *infra*). Even in higher latitudes the adult has been most frequently recorded either from considerable depths, or as dead and floating if at the surface.—G. H. F.]

[*Note added Aug.* 1898 —The stages shown in figs. 5 & 6 are connected by an intermediate specimen of 7·5 mm., received too late for description in the text. The proportions of the head, eye, and snout are as in the specimen of 8 mm., but the general form is more slender.—E. W. L. H.]

IMPERFECTLY CHARACTERIZED LARVA with very elongate abdomen. ? MALLOTUS VILLOSUS Muller. Capelin. (Plate XLVII. figs. 8-11.)

These very elongate larvæ have at first sight much the appearance of young Eels, but closer inspection soon dispels this illusion. They measure respectively 17, 19 (*ca.*), and 24·5 mm., from the snout to the extremity of the notochord. I have figured the most advanced, which on the whole is the most perfect specimen of the series. The others differ little in general conformation, but the smallest has the caudal extremity still practically diphycercal, and the marginal fin terminates, without spatulate expansion, in a sharp lanciform process. The proportionate lengths of the abdominal and caudal regions are shown in Plate XLVII. fig. 8; it will be seen that the abdomen is about twice as long as the tail, the rectum being thus given off at a point far posterior to median. The fore-brain extends but little in front of the eye, which is only of moderate proportions The considerable bluntly-rounded rostral region is occupied anteriorly by a large olfactory pouch. The angle of the jaws is opposite the front of the eye. The pectorals are small. The pelvics are indicated by a pair of membranous lobes supported anteriorly by a thickened fleshy rim. They are situate at about the middle of the total length of the larva, and well behind the middle of the abdominal region The liver occurs as a small pyriform mass shortly behind the clavicle. The alimentary canal, apparently wide and thin-walled in the thoracic region, is soon constricted and thickened. Its ventral wall shows a downward crenulation (about halfway between the clavicle and the pelvics) which may be accidental. At the pelvic region commences a well-marked intestinal tract lined with transverse (annular, perhaps spiral) ridges. The short and rather voluminous rectum leaves the trunk in an oblique direction.

There are 47 abdominal (counted to the origin of the rectum) and 20 caudal myomeres visible: others may probably be seen at a later stage, but the total number will not be much greater than 67. Black pigment is present in a series of ventral spots, seven in number, distributed at regular intervals from the clavicular region backward These consist for the most part of a single chromatophore on either side of the gut, but at the shoulder there are several, as also at the region of the rectal valve. The pre-peduncular spot of the tail consists of two ventral and one lateral chromatophore. The caudal fin, both as to the embryonic and permanent parts, is rather profusely decorated with small black dots. The eyes are deeply pigmented. The dorsal marginal fin is wide. Anteriorly it is rather imperfect in the specimen figured. In that of about 19 mm. the fin appears to be ampullate anteriorly, and this is probably the natural condition in the others also. There are no signs of the permanent dorsal and anal fins, but embryonic rays occur in the postanal region

On comparison of the three examples it would appear that the ventral spots become reduced as development advances. Though identical in number those of the largest individual are relatively considerably smaller than those of the younger.

I have noticed elsewhere (p 565 *infra*) the occurrence in Dr. Fowler's collection of a pelagic egg, which, as far as may be judged from the preserved condition, appears to be practically identical with Raffaele's species No 7 (Mitth. zool. Stat. Neap viii. 1888, p. 69) In conformation and in distribution of pigment the form which we are now dealing with bears a striking likeness to the larva of Sp. 7 (*op. cit.* tav. v. fig. 9). The ventral spots are numerically equal, and there is an indication in the Faeroe larva of the large "rhomboidal ' supra-cephalic sinus described in Sp. 7. The latter is stated to have 59 or 60 abdominal segments, a condition which indicates that the total number is considerably in excess of that present in the much more advanced Faeroe larva, and so disposes of the possibility of the formula being harmonized in the two forms by a developmental migration of the anus. The marginal fin, though wider in the Faeroe larvæ, terminates, in the youngest example, as in Sp. 7; and in the anterior dorsal region appears to be inflated alike in both forms. But none of the Faeroe larvæ show any trace of the prodigious buccal armature of Sp. 7. The teeth, on the contrary are quite small.

Sp. 7 is one of a group of ova and larvæ which Raffaele considered to exhibit Murænoid affinities; and Grassi has practically confirmed the correctness of this view in the case of at least one species, No. 10, which he has connected with *Anguilla vulgaris*. Moreover it appears probable that all Murænid larvæ pass through a *Leptocephalus*-stage, losing the buccal armature of what Grassi terms the pre-larval condition. I imagine that it is impossible to connect the Faeroe larvæ with either end of a Leptocephaline metamorphosis; while the condition of the intestine and the caudal fin suggest for them affinities which are not Murænoid. The presence of pelvic fins can hardly be held to prove that they are not Murænoids; at least until Grassi shall have found that such structures never occur as vestigial phenomena in the development of Eels [1].

In 1893 my friend Captain F Klotz, s.s 'Dominican,' brought me a number of young fish which he had taken at the surface off the West Horn of Iceland on the 27th July. They range in size from 36 to 57 mm., and in general shape have much the appearance of Sand-eels (*Ammodytes*). The collection is sufficiently serial to show that only one species is present, while the largest appear to associate themselves with the Capelin, *Mallotus villosus*. I have figured the head of the smallest (fig. 9), a specimen of 42.5 mm. (fig 10), and the largest (fig. 11). The radial formula of the largest appears to be D. 12 (or a few more), A. 21. This specimen has 64 myomeres (perhaps more, as the pectoral region is lacerated) exclusive of the peduncular part of the tail, where a few others are probably present, though not sufficiently defined to be counted. About 49 are abdominal. From the ocular region backward the head is distinctly trigonal in section, the upper surface being flat while the sides approach each other ventrally. Though this is rather less marked in the buccal region, there is a distinct approach to the conformation (a three-sided pyramid) described by Smitt (Hist Scand. Fish. ed 2, p. 877) as characteristic of the head of the adult Capelin The sides of the body are compressed and flattened, while the dorsum is also rather flat *Mallotus* has the radial formula D. 12–16, A. 18–25; the vertebræ are from 65 to 70. In general proportions and in the relative position of the fins the oldest Iceland specimen is in agreement with *Mallotus* (compare Smitt's figures of the latter, *op. cit.* pl. xli. with my figure 11). The Iceland specimens are a good deal damaged and none have any scales on the body, but there are traces of them on the gill-cover of the largest. The teeth are small, and there is no distinct notch in the premaxillary region for the reception of the mandibular extremity.

Beyond a few remarks of Collett's, quoted by Smitt, I have not found any description of the young stages of *Mallotus*. Our

---

[1] Lütken ("Spol Atlant , Changements de forme chez les Poissons," Vid Selsk. Skr 5 Række, 1880, p 594) considers that pelvic fins probably exist in the young of all species of *Trichiurus*, though their presence is only indicated in the adult of one species.

Iceland forms show a certain resemblance to the genera *Paralepis*
and *Sudis*. *Paralepis borealis* is known from Greenland, Iceland,
and the North-American coast. Apart from other differences, the
excessive number of anal rays and the large size of the teeth (*vide*
Goode & Bean, Ocean. Ichth. p. 119, fig 143) serve to separate
it from the forms before us. *P. coregonoides* has occurred in the
Mediterranean and on the American Atlantic coast, and may well
exist in Boreal European waters. It appears to agree better than
the last with the Iceland forms, but has the generic character of
very large teeth. *P. sphyrænoides*, from the Mediterranean and
Madeira, has 30 anal rays. I cannot ascertain the vertebral
formula of any of these species. Under the name of *Sudis
atlanticus* Smitt gives a brief account, derived from Kroyer, of
a fish washed ashore at the Skaw. It had 20 anal rays, and so
far as I can judge its young stage might bear some resemblance to
the Iceland specimens. The balance of probability, however,
appears to me to favour the association of the latter with *Mallotus
villosus* [1], although, so far as I know, the Capelin has never been
recorded from Iceland.

The smallest Iceland specimens bear a considerable resemblance
to the largest of Dr. Fowler's larvæ. In the latter (fig. 8) the
snout is obtuse and rounded except at the extremity. In the
former (fig. 9) the snout is more pointed, but still somewhat
rounded superiorly. A depression behind the eyes indicates the
collapse of a sinus over the hind-brain, such as seems to have been
also present in the Faeroe larvæ. The specimen 36 mm. long has
the greatest height of the body only 2·5 mm. ; the form being thus
extremely elongate. The gradual increase in height is illustrated
in figs. 10 and 11.

Most of the Iceland forms have only a few chromatophores
scattered along the ventral surface, but one, about 42 mm., has a
number rather widely diffused over the general surface of the head
and body. How far the generally unpigmented condition is
natural I cannot say.

A size-interval of 11·5 mm. separates the largest of the Faeroe
larvæ from the smallest of the Iceland series. Since in the former
the isolated spots of the ventrum appear to be in process of
reduction, their absence in the latter is not necessarily a bar to
the association of two series. The Faeroe larvæ have certainly a
a smaller eye than the Iceland forms, but we have evidence of a
developmental increase in the size of this organ in *Scopelus* which
may well be repeated in other fishes of similar environment. In
the Iceland series the proportions of the eye are variable, but in
the larger and more perfect examples an increase is associated

---

[1] Dr Gunther considers that a number of larval forms, corresponding to
Richardson's genus *Prymnothonus* (*vide* Chall Rep, Zool xxxi Pelag Fish p 39,
pl v), "represent larval conditions of fishes belonging to *Paralepis* or *Sudis* or
of genera allied to them" I venture to suggest that in the genera named the
abdomen will be found to be much more elongate, from the earliest stages, than
in *Prymnothonus*

with advance of general development. In the number of myomeres both Faeroe and Iceland forms agree well enough with *Mallotus*.

The latter has not been recorded from any point nearer to the Faeroe Channel than the coast of Norway, but appears to be a fish of pelagic habit, approaching the coast only for the purpose of spawning. The ova are demersal, and it may be objected that our Faeroe larvæ are too young to be found so far from land. This objection depends for its validity on a knowledge of the rate of growth, which is not forthcoming.

Although I think I have demonstrated the possibility of connecting the Faeroe larvæ, through intermediate stages as represented by the Iceland series, with the adult form of *Mallotus villosus*, I do not think we are justified in considering the question settled. The fact is that we know next to nothing of the development of many marine forms and especially of the pelagic and bathybial species, nor can it be supposed likely that a few sporadic cruises have furnished us with an even approximately complete list of the fish-fauna of the Faeroe Channel. In all probability there is a strong resemblance between the larvæ of many physostomous fishes, however widely they may be separated in the adult condition. Of the method of reproduction of bathybial fishes, whether by pelagic or demersal ova, we are in most cases ignorant. The characters of the Faeroe larva, though probably sufficient to exclude it from the Murænidæ, are such as might occur equally in a Salmonoid, Scopeloid, or Clupeoid. Any Clupeoids known as inhabitants of the region may be eliminated, since we know the larval stages of all of them. The same remark applies, as I think, to *Argentina sphyræna*, specimens of 37 mm. have already acquired the adult conformation[1], though only about 13 mm. longer than the Faeroe example, which is still practically undifferentiated. The size-interval does not appear sufficient, and I imagine that this species of *Argentina* has a shorter larva, with, of course, fewer myomeres. *A. silus* has 65 to 68 vertebræ and is a much larger fish. It may conceivably pass through a larval stage like the Faeroe form if its pelvic fins undergo an anterior migration. Among the Scopeloids *Stomias* is an elongate form, and *S. ferox* has been recorded by Gunther from the Faeroe Channel (Chall. xxxi. *op. cit.* p. 31).

However, the example in question, though capable of even specific determination, was again only 37 mm in length; while I can find in the Faeroe larva of 24·5 mm. no trace of the barbel and enlarged teeth of *Stomias*. I have already referred to the characters of the *Paralepidæ*, and the enumeration might be prolonged but always without bringing us, for the present, any nearer to a definite conclusion.

Dr. Fowler's specimens were taken as follows :—

13 *i*. 60° 2' N., 5° 49' W. 100 to 0 fathoms. Two, 19 and 24·5 mm.

20 *c*. 60° 16' N., 5° 49' W. 400 to 300 fathoms. One, 17 mm.

[1] Holt & Calderwood, Trans R. Dubl Soc ser. 2, v 1895, p. 509, fig J

If they prove to be young *Mallotus* it will have been shown that form is capable of descending below the 300-fathom line. The localities are just outside the British area

A PELAGIC EGG, resembling Raffaele's species No. 7.

⁹ Raffaele, Mittheil zool. Stat. Neap viii. 1888, p. 69, tav. 5. Undetermined species no. 7.

Dr. Fowler's collection contains only one egg, which is quite unlike any that has been recorded from British or Northern European coasts. Preserved in a weak solution of formaldehyde, it was not sufficiently transparent for an exact determination of the internal structure. It was therefore passed through the usual reagents into oil of cloves, a process which unfortunately involved a complete collapse of the zona radiata. An attempt to remove the latter without injury to the contents was only partially successful. The characters, as observed during the whole process of manipulation, appear to be as follow :—

The diameter is 3·5 mm , the shape approximately spherical. The zona is thin and probably without any distinctive feature, since some bubble-like markings present on one part appear to be due to the adherence of a thin layer of yolk-matter. The peri-vitelline space is certainly large, but the exact dimensions of the yolk had been obscured by rupture either in the net or by the action of formaldehyde. The embryo remains attached to a pyriform yolk-mass 1·19 mm. by ·90 mm., the narrow end under-lying the head. The yolk is divided throughout into small rounded segments of irregular size, and appeared to possess, as seen in formaldehyde, a number of small oil-globules aggregated together. The embryo is advanced and has a considerable free tail, closely apposed to the yolk. Its total length may be estimated at about 2·40 mm. There appears to be no pigment. Any distinctive characters which may have been present could not be observed before the removal of the zona, and the specimen was too much injured in this process to admit of a reliable observation of the embryo.

Sufficient, however, has been noted to show that the egg agrees very closely, both in dimensions and other characters, with Raffaele's species no 7. Grassi's researches[1] have confirmed Raffaele's suggestion of a Muraenoid parentage for at least some of the group of evidently allied ova to which no. 7 belongs, one of them, no 10, having been connected in a practically conclusive manner with the Common Eel (*Anguilla vulgaris*).

No observer has yet described the perfectly ripe egg of the Conger (*C vulgaris*), nor has any attempt been made to identify with this abundant and rather valuable form any egg taken in the tow-net. It appears from Cunningham's description (Q. J. M. S. xl. p 155) that the ripe egg probably differs from that of *Anguilla* in possessing one or more oil-globules, and therein agrees with Raffaele's sp. 7 and with the egg from the

[1] Q J M S xxix p 371

Faeroe Channel.   In eggs characterized by a large perivitelline
space, such as those of *Hippoglossoides* and some species of *Clupea*,
the expansion of the zona is known to be accomplished after
deposition.   The difference of dimension of the yolk-mass, as
between sp. 7, the Faeroe Channel egg, and the largest eggs
obtained by Cunningham from the Conger[1], does not appear to be
considerable.   The specific identity of the three appears at least .
possible

On the other hand, it may well be that Raffaele's group of eggs
belongs in fact to more than one family of physostomous fishes.
I have described from Dr. Fowler's collection a series of larvæ,
which are apparently not Eels, but which in conformation and
pigment agree rather closely with the larva of Raffaele's no 7,
though they entirely lack the peculiar buccal armature of the
latter.   Such armature is, in the Eels, a very temporary pheno-
menon, the leptocephaline condition being devoid of it.

To attempt to connect the Faeroe egg with the elongate larva
from the same region were simply an unprofitable speculation :
but it may be suggested that the characters of segmented yolk
and large perivitelline space, common to Muraenidæ and Clupeidæ,
may be equally present in the ova of Scopeloids and of such, if
any, Salmonoids as propagate by means of pelagic eggs.   In point
of attenuation I know no larvæ more eel-like than some of the
Clupeoids   I do not suppose that the egg with which we are
dealing is that of a Clupeoid, but, whether it be identical with
Raffaele's no. 7, or different, our knowledge of the development
of the pelagic and bathybial members of the other groups
mentioned is hardly such as to permit us to definitely assign it to
any one of them.   *Mallotus*, which I have suggested as a possible
parent of the elongate larva, is known to deposit ova which are
demersal in littoral waters.   If any description of their structure
exists I have not seen it.

EXPLANATION OF THE PLATES
PLATE XLVI

Fig. 1 *Scopelus glacialis*, 14 5 mm , p 552   Formol
    2.   „   „   12 mm. Formol
    3.   „   „   11 5 mm. Formol   The larval sinus in front of
                                the dorsal fin rather collapsed
    4 Dorsal view of the same specimen. Formol
    5 *S glacialis*, 8 mm. Oil of cloves

PLATE XLVII

Fig 6 *S glacialis*, 6 5 mm , p 552   Oil of cloves.
    7   „   „   4 5 mm   Oil of cloves
    8 Larva with elongate abdomen, 24 5 mm , p 560   Oil of cloves
    9 Head of young *Mallotus villosus?*, 36 mm , p 560   From Iceland
            Alcohol
    10 Young *M villosus?*, 42 5 mm p 560. From Iceland   Alcohol
    11   „   „   57 mm   From Iceland. Alcohol   Natural size
    12 Young *Gadus æglefinus*, 8 mm , p 551. Formol

_____

[1] *Cf* Journ M B A , n s ii. 1891, pp 24 25

6. Contributions to our Knowledge of the Plankton of the Faeroe Channel.—No. VI.[1]   Description of a new Mid-water Tow-net.   Discussion of the Mid-water Fauna (Mesoplankton).   Notes on *Doliolum tritonis* and *D. nationalis*, and on *Parathemisto abyssorum*.   By G. Herbert Fowler, B A , Ph.D., Assistant Professor of Zoology, University College, London.

[Received June 18, 1898]

In the first paper of this series, I proposed to leave the description of the mid-water nets used, and the discussion of the general question of the existence of a mid-water fauna or Mesoplankton, until the collections made on the ' Research ' had been thoroughly investigated.   The net which I used last year proved so successful in actual working, that it now seems to me better to describe it at once for the information of other investigators, who might give it a further trial, the more so since my leisure for research work is but small. and the collections cannot be completely finished for some months to come.

It is unnecessary to describe here the numerous and varied forms of apparatus which have been devised for the capture of animals at known mid-water depths without admixture of the fauna from other zones.   References to them will be found, by those interested, in the papers of Hoyle[2], H.H. the Prince of Monaco[3], and Agassiz[4]; since the appearance of the last-named, a full description of the ' National ' apparatus has been published by Hensen[5]. Agassiz, in the paper cited. has subjected the earlier forms of net to a searching criticism, with which I agree on the whole ; except that of the Prince of Monaco and that of the ' National,' none appear to exclude satisfactorily animals from undesirable zones. Even that of the Prince of Monaco does not appear to have worked satisfactorily on the ' Pola '; and the modification of Chun's net used on the ' National ' was uncertain in its action[6].

When desirous to study for myself the question of a mid-water fauna or Mesoplankton[6], I feared that both the nets last quoted were too expensive, and the ' National ' net too complicated for use in such heavy seas as are generally to be found in the Faeroe Channel, the only deep-water readily accessible to me.   Returning therefore to Chun's[7] original ingenious design as a starting

For Part I , see P Z S 1896, p 991 , Part II , P Z S 1897, p 523 , Part III , P Z S 1897, p 803 , Part IV , *antea*, p 540 , Part V , *antea*, p. 550
- Proc Liverpool Biol Soc iii. 100
[3] CR Congrès international de Zoologie, Paris, 1889, p. 133
[4] Bull Mus Comp Zool Harvard, xxiii 1
[5] Ergebnisse d. Plankton Exped. Methodik der Untersuchungen p 103 *et seqq* (1895)
[6] For the explanation of this and similar new terms used here, see p 545 *ante*.
[7] C Chun Bibliotheca Zoologica, i 1

point, I endeavoured to introduce into it such improvements as would obviate what appeared to me to be its weaknesses, namely · (1) The position of the wires when the net had shut, which necessitate the mouth being always slightly open ; (2) the lack of power to keep the net-mouth shut in a roll of the ship or a check on the line, as the attachments of the wires by which it then hangs are so close together ; (3) the speed at which the whole structure must be towed in order that the screw-propeller, and the rod to which it is fixed, may overcome the frictional resistance offered by the rings on which the weight of the net is hanging.

I decided to construct a net for vertical and not for horizontal use, because it seems to me, on the basis of my small experience, impossible to be certain of the depth at which a net is being towed horizontally. The usual method for this is to lower the net vertically, and to begin towing with the rope straight up and down , then to observe the angle made by the rope with the horizon by means of a quadrant, and to calculate the vertical depth of the net by traverse tables on the assumption that the towing-line is the hypotenuse of a right-angled triangle. Unfortunately for this method, however, the towing-rope is not a hypotenuse, but forms an unknown catenary, which varies with the weight of the net, its resistance to the water, and the pace of towing ; this forms an increasing source of error, the greater is the length of towing-warp out. As an example of the uncertainty of this method,—I struck bottom at 398 fathoms in the Faeroe Channel, when by quadrant and traverse tables the net should have been at 300 fathoms with 450 fathoms of rope out. There are so many forces at work as to make it impossible for any but a highly skilled mathematician to calculate the probable position of the net, and this only after tedious experiment.

Description of the Apparatus

This consists of the net, the net-frame and chains, and the locking-gear. As the first of these were used both in 1896 and 1897, they will be described in detail ; the locking-gear of the 1896 pattern will only be sufficiently sketched to enable future workers in this field to profit by my experience of failures, the 1897 pattern will be fully described.

The **net** is made of Swiss Silk Boulting Cloth, by far the best material known to zoologists for every form of tow-net; it was supplied by Messrs. Staniar of the Manchester Wire Works ; this material will stand almost any fair pull, but, as it is very liable to be cut by anything sharp, when coming inboard, the actual net is surrounded by a loose case of common mosquito-netting. A net with a twenty-inch square mouth, tapered to a four-inch diameter cod-end, and six feet in length, was found to be a good working size. It should be sewn throughout by hand, not by machine; and with strong sewing-silk, not thread. If washed nightly in fresh water and dried in the air, a net of this sort will last for a very long time.

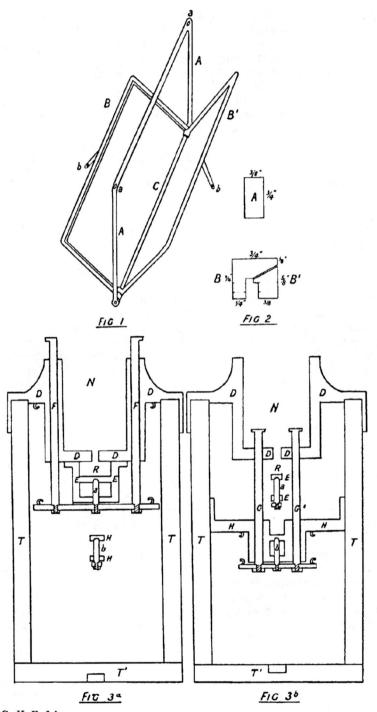

FIG 1

FIG 2

FIG 3ᵃ

FIG 3ᵇ

G H T del

As a mid-water net has to be drawn up by a steam-winch more rapidly than is usual with a surface tow-net, even when the winch is going its slowest, boulting cloth of twenty-five (1896) and forty (1897) meshes to the inch was selected, of these the second is stronger and more efficient   If the winding-drum can be run dead slow by gearing, 50 or even 60 meshes to the inch might be used. A calico band at the mouth pierced by lacing-holes, and a calico band at the cod-end, with a tape by which the collecting zinc pot is tied in, complete the net.   The tape should run in loops *outside* the calico band, it is there much easier to untie with cold wet fingers.

The **net-frame** (fig. 1, where it is represented as half open) consists of two ⌐ shaped phosphor-bronze castings **BB'** hinged together on a solid brass axle **C**, on to the latter is also hinged, outside **BB'**, a wrought iron ⌐ shaped piece **A**, which is rather larger than the other two.   The arms **bb** of **BB'** are drilled to take shackle-bolts from which chains pass upward to the locking-gear, two holes are also drilled at **aa** for similar shackle-bolts and chains The net-frame in its descent is suspended from **bb**, and is therefore tightly closed by its own weight (about 15 lbs.) and by any additional weight that may be hung on the axle, the arms pressing **BB'** firmly together ; when the chains from **bb** are slacked by the locking-gear, the net falls for a short distance, the weight is caught on to the chains from **aa**, and the net-mouth either falls open, or opens on the slightest pull in towing.   The whole apparatus is then hauled upwards through the zone which it is desired to investigate (generally 100 fathoms)   The chains from **aa** are then slacked by the locking-gear, the net falls a second time, and the weight, being caught on the chains from **bb**, again closes the net effectively

In fig. 2 the sectional dimensions of **A, B, B'** are given, the net-frame being represented as closed   The upper end of the net itself, laced inside the frame, is compressed into the space between **B** and **B'**; the dotted lines indicate the lacing-holes drilled through the frame at intervals of an inch.   When it is closed, only a Protozoan could get through the net-mouth, and even that would find a difficulty.—**B** and **B'** when open form a mouth twenty inches square (inside measurement); **A** is $\frac{3}{4}$ inch outside them when closed. The arms **bb** are seven inches long, and effect a good leverage for closing the net   They form one of the most important improvements on the original pattern.   Even shaking the frame violently up and down when held by the chains does not open the net.

[The **locking-gear** of the 1896 pattern was arranged as follows — Through the chains from **aa** and **bb** were passed the hammers of two reversed gun-lock movements, the hammer rising when fired ; the lock of the **bb** chains was placed vertically below that of the **aa** chains.   Parallel to the vertical between these two ran a long steel rod, tapped with a screw-thread : at the lower end of the steel rod was a screw-propeller, arranged so as not to revolve during the descent of the apparatus.   When hauled upwards, however, the propeller began to revolve, travelled up the steel rod, and fired the trigger of the lower lock-movement, thus slackening the bb chains and allowing the net frame to fall open; still travelling upwards, as the apparatus was hauled in, the propeller presently fired the trigger of the upper lock-movement, slacked the aa chains, and the net then closed. The whole apparatus was prevented from spinning in its descent, and thus causing the propeller to begin travelling too soon, by being suspended from a swivel which worked on ball-bearings.

This arrangement worked successfully in about three hauls out of four, the failures being generally due to one or both chains hanging on the hammer, even when the lock-movement had been fired, owing to the great friction of the chains on the hammers. A further disadvantage in the apparatus was the difficult adjustment of the distance between the triggers, which determined the distance in fathoms for which the net remained open; this further had a tendency to vary somewhat with the rate of hauling in.]

In designing the **locking-gear** of the 1897 pattern I therefore abandoned the propeller in favour of messengers, which I had originally avoided on the grounds of others' experience with the light messengers of deep-sea thermometers. There seems, however, to be no objection to the use of *heavy* messengers on any well-stretched rope (hemp or wire) which hangs free of the bottom, and in which kinks are thus avoided by the maintenance of a steady strain

Photographs of the whole apparatus are given on page 572. Details of the locking-gear are furnished by figs. 3 a, 3 b (p 569), which are sectional drawings at right angles to one another. They are carefully drawn to scale, about one-seventh of the real size.

Four vertical pillars of teak [1] **T**, connected below by two cross-pieces of the same material **T'**, and strengthened by iron plates at the angles, form a rigid frame; on to this is screwed a brass casting **D**, to which a second casting **E** is screwed   The rope by which the machine is slung passes through a hole in the centre of **D** into the space R between **D** and **E**, and is kept there by being worked into a broad knot.

Two brass cylindrical rods or pins **FF** (fig 3 a) run in two good bearings through **D** and are rigidly bolted into a cross-piece which carries a third shorter pin **a**, travelling in bearings through the centre of **E**. The pin **a** is passed through the chains from aa on the net-frame, and is kept in place by springs (not drawn) between the hooks shown in fig. 3 a with a pull of about 10 lbs. If a weight be dropped on to the pins **FF**, it will overcome the springs, depress the pin **a**, and let go the chains from aa.

A second pair of pins **GG** (fig. 3 b) run in bearings through **D**, and through another casting **H** which is bolted to **TT**. They are rigidly bolted to a cross-piece which carries a third pin **b**, travelling in bearings through the centre of **H**, this pin is passed through

[1] Teak is one of the few woods that will resist the enormous pressure at great depths, less closely grained woods warp and split.

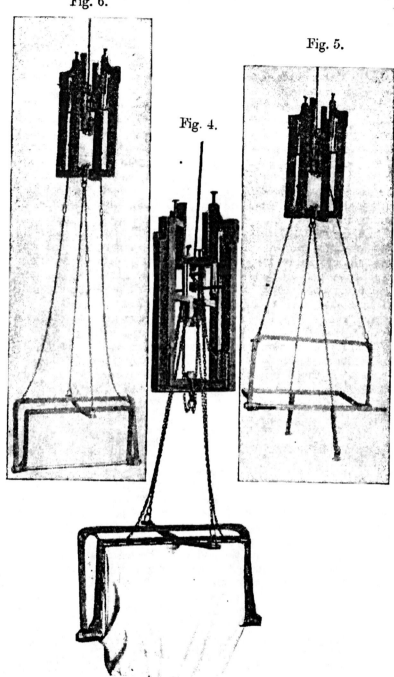

Fig. 6.

Fig. 5.

Fig. 4.

the chains from bb on the arms of the net-frame, and is kept in place by springs (rubber loops) between the hooks shown in fig. 3 b, with a pull of about 10 lbs. If a weight be dropped on to the pins **GG**, it will overcome the springs, depress the the pin **b**, and let go the chains from **bb**.

The apparatus is worked thus :—The whole machine is lowered with the locking-gear in the position drawn in figure 4, the chains **aa** held on the pin a, but not carrying the weight of the net and frame ; the chains **bb** held on the pin b, and holding the net-frame tightly closed by its own weight. When the machine is at the bottom of the zone which it is desired to study, the first messenger is despatched down the rope, this, being small, drops into the nest **N**, striking on the pins **GG**, and freeing the chains **bb** ; the net-frame falls 6 inches, and opens, the weight being caught with a jerk on the chains **aa**.

The machine in this condition (fig. 5) is hauled upwards for a hundred fathoms ; the second and larger messenger is despatched, which, striking on the pins **FF**, frees the chains aa ; the net falls 15 inches, the weight is caught again on the chains **bb** ; the net-frame closes, and can be then hauled in-board without any admixture with the fauna of higher zones (fig. 6).

The chains of course are not let go altogether, as the net and frame would then be lost, each chain has a large link in it to go over its pin, and beyond this a short length by which it is bolted to **T** or a shackle-bolt in the centre of **T'**.

	Chains aa.	Chains bb.
From net-frame to pin.. ...	33 in	23 in.
From pin to T	9 5 in.	. .
From pin to central bolt of T'	. .	12 in.

The messengers used in 1897 were clumsy and unnecessarily heavy, and will not be described here. Probably weights of 4 lbs. for the smaller and 6 lbs for the larger are amply sufficient on rope : smaller weights would do on wire, since the friction is less.

The apparatus was tested in 1897 on H.M.S. 'Research,' but, unfortunately, owing to heavy weather, we were only able to spend one day in the deep water of the Faroe Channel, the apparatus was tried four times, and seemed to work perfectly. The only improvement which suggested itself was that a weight should be hung from the axle **C** into the middle of the net, heavy enough to prevent the net in its descent from washing up into the machinery (which happened once, but without serious consequences) ; the additional weight at this point will also serve to shut the net-mouth more closely, and can also be arranged to prevent the sides of the net compressing the contents when closed. Should the first messenger strike **FF** before **GG**, the net would simply come up empty, having been open only for a few seconds.

Weight of net-frame 16½ lbs. ; of locking-gear and chains 33 lbs. ; of messengers used in 1897 (7½ + 10) 17½ lbs. ; of messengers for future use $(4+6)$ 10 lbs ; suggested above to be added at $T' T'$, 10 lbs., and to be hung on C, 10 lbs. : total about 80 lbs.

At the conclusion of the four hauls, the net was sent down to 100 fathoms, and hauled up without the messengers having been despatched ; it came up empty, although it had passed through the stratum where life was probably most plentiful. I am unable to see any source of error in the working of this apparatus, but hope that it may be given a further trial before long [1]. Of course, with an apparatus half a mile away from one in water, one cannot see what is actually occurring ; one can only take precautions against every possible source of error, and may judge of their success to some extent by the character of the animals obtained.

Conclusions of Prof. Agassiz the Azoic Zone.

In discussing the general results of the ' Albatross ' Expedition in 1891 [2], Prof. Agassiz reviewed the apparatus used and conclusions attained by earlier naturalists who had attempted a solution of the question of a Mesoplankton. His own views are based on experiments made during the cruises of the ' Blake ' (1877–80) and the ' Albatross ' (1891). On the first of these vessels he used the gravitating-trap [3] invented by Lieutenant-Commander (now Captain) Sigsbee, which not only failed to catch living organisms between 100 and 150 fathoms, but apparently missed even the corpses of the dead surface fauna ! The machine is only stated to have been tried on two occasions, and only to a depth of 150 fathoms, from this Agassiz concluded [4] (p 37) that "these experiments serve to prove that the pelagic fauna does not extend to considerable depths, and that there is at sea an immense intermediate belt in which no living animals are found, nothing but the dead bodies which are on their way to the bottom." On the ' Albatross ' a new apparatus was tried, the invention of Captain Tanner, which is fully described and figured by Prof. Agassiz. On the basis of this he states [4] (p 55).—" Our experience in the Gulf of California with the Tanner self-closing net would seem to indicate that in a comparatively closed sea, at a small distance from the land, there may be a mixture of the surface species with the free-swimming deep sea bottom species, a condition of things which certainly does not exist at sea, in deep water, in an oceanic basin at a great distance from shore, where the surface pelagic fauna only

[1] The cost of the apparatus should come to about £10, now that the patterns for casting have been made If any zoologist will give it a further trial, I shall be glad to superintend its manufacture

Since the above was written, my net has been taken for a further trial by the German Expedition which sailed on August 1st under Prof Chun's direction, and Prof. Max Weber has ordered a net for the Dutch East-Indian Expedition

[2] Bull. Mus Comp Zool. Harvard, xxiii. 1

[3] Bull Mus. Comp Zool. Harvard, xiv 36 (=' Three Cruises of the Blake,' vol i p 36, London. 1888, 8vo)

[4] Bull Mus. Comp Zool Harvard, xxiii. 1.

descends to a comparatively small depth, _i. e._ about 200 fathoms, the limits of the depth at which light and heat produce any considerable variation in the physical conditions of the water   The marked diminution in the number of species below 200 fathoms agrees fairly with the results of the ' National' Expedition."

The other experiments with the Tanner net, made in an oceanic basin on the way to Acapulco from the Galapagos, and to the Galapagos from Cape San Francisco, " seem to prove conclusively that in the open sea, even when close to the land, the surface pelagic fauna does not descend far beyond a depth of 200 fathoms, and that there is no intermediate pelagic fauna living between that depth and the bottom, and that even the free-swimming bottom-species do not rise to any great distance, as we found no trace of anything within 60 fathoms from the bottom, where it had been fairly populated."

Prof. Agassiz therefore admits the existence of a deep Meso-plankton near land, but does not state how far from land and in what depth of water his generalization of an Azoic zone begins to hold good.   I do not know of any later pronouncement by this eminent oceanographer on the question.   Since then, Captain Tanner has improved his original pattern in detail [1], but the principle of his net remains the same.   It is rash, and perhaps a little ungracious, to criticize the working of a net which one has never seen ; but I venture to suggest, on the basis of the drawings and description of the Tanner nets, that a weak point in them is the way in which the tripping lines are suspended ; it seems that it would be so very easy for them to slip off from the tumbler and close the net before they were intended to do so, under the alternate strain and slackening of the warp as the ship rolls ; it also seems likely, and indeed Captain Tanner himself admits, that the angle made sometimes by the net-frame in turning would practically close the net's mouth.   As regards the Sigsbee gravitating trap, there can, I think, be little doubt that it was too small and too violent to throw much light on the question of an Azoic zone.

Conclusions of the ' Challenger' and other Naturalists. the Mesoplankton.

Prof. Agassiz may be regarded as the chief representative of the school of naturalists which refuses to accept the alleged existence of a Mesoplankton.   The chief supporters of the opposite view are the ' Challenger' naturalists (a distinguished band, of whom Sir John Murray is alone left), Prof. Chun, and Profs. Hensen and Brandt of the ' National' staff.

The ' Challenger' naturalists arrived at their belief from a comparison of serial tow-nets, stopped at intervals along the dredge-rope.   As all the tow-nets were open throughout their course, the presence of particular species in the deep nets only seemed to indicate that these species occurred in the deep water only.   The

[1] Z. L. Tanner, Bull. U S. Fish Commission, xiv. p. 148.

method is theoretically excellent [1], but is not certain enough for use as an argument against the negative observations of the 'Blake' and 'Albatross.'

While I am fully in agreement with Professor Chun's results, it must be admitted that the original pattern of his net was not devoid of sources of error, which Agassiz was not slow to point out. Chun reported [2] an abundant fauna from all depths in the Mediterranean, but, this being a warm closed sea with a uniform temperature of 55° or 56° F. from 100 down to 2400 fathoms and more, no thermal barriers are here set to the vertical descent of an organism. It is not therefore possible to argue from this case to that of the great oceans, the temperature of which decreases with the depth until 30° F. or even less is reached.

Three hauls made by Prof. Chun on a voyage to the Canary Islands [3] revealed a Mesoplankton at great depths, the general character of which agreed with the similar captures of the 'Challenger' and 'National.' The net used was an improvement on the Mediterranean pattern: open nets were also employed in other hauls.

As regards the 'National' net, a modification of Chun's pattern, Prof. Agassiz expressed suspicion of the locking arrangement which closed it. Prof Brandt was kind enough to show it to me some years ago in Kiel; it is extremely ingenious in mechanism, but, as Prof. Hensen [4] admits, it is most uncertain in its action; and, if I may judge from my own experience of a screw-propeller, it would not give very exact information of the depth; for the rate at which the propeller travels (i. e. the time-intervals from first hauling to opening, and from opening to shutting) varies so much with the rate of the steam-winch (an inconstant) and with the rolling of the ship. If there is any swell, the strain on the line as the ship rolls to leeward sends the propeller round at a greatly increased rate. While, however, venturing to criticize the method, I accept the positive results without any reserve, so far as they are published. They have been most recently summarized by Prof. Brandt [5], and show a mesoplanktonic fauna which rapidly diminishes in numbers below 100 fathoms, together with a large number of dead organisms which are slowly settling to the bottom. Prof. Hensen [6]

[1] Though theoretically perfect and simple, this method of investigating Mesoplankton appears to me to present two practical objections to its use· the one, that such an enormous amount of material must be collected as will take years for its proper identificaiton, before a comparison of surface and deep nets can be instituted, the other, that much of the deep material must inevitably be reduced to soup by pressure against the open tow-net in its long passage upwards, only forms with a strong skeleton (Radiolaria, Copepoda, &c) can be expected to arrive fairly unbroken In a closed net the resistance of the water does not appear to press the contents of the net against the meshes in the same way

[2] C Chun Biblhotheca Zoologica, i

[3] C. Chun Biblhotheca Zoologica, vii., and SB Akad Beln 1889, p 519.

[4] V. Hensen, Ergebn d. Plankton Expedition, Methodik der Untersuchungen, p. 106

[5] K Brandt Verh Gesellsch. deutschen Naturforscher und Aertze fur 1895, Lubeck, p. 107.

[6] V Hensen: Reisebeschreibung der Plankton Expedition, p. 28.

maintains the accurate locking of his net as against Prof. Agassiz's criticism, and makes a very pregnant remark on the point .—" Das Netz ist aber nur das Mittel um beweisende Fänge möglichst rein zu erhalten, der wirkliche Beweis ist die Beschaffenheit des Fanges "

The above summary represents briefly the results and conclusions of the chief writers who have studied the question experimentally : in the case of Prof. Agassiz, negative results have led to the assertion of an Azoic zone ; in the case of the 'Challenger,' the 'National,' and Prof. Chun, positive observations have led to the conclusion of the existence of a Mesoplankton, but in these cases the mechanism of locking the net has not been sufficiently certain to escape the criticisms of the opponent school.   With their results the less extensive experiments of the Prince of Monaco ('l'Hirondelle'), the 'Pola,' and the 'Gazelle' are in general accord.

Results of the Cruises of the 'Research,' 1896 and 1897.

In commencing to work at this question, I attempted to construct a locking-gear with which not even Prof. Agassiz could find fault , with the view, firstly, of finally settling the question of the existence of a Mesoplankton, secondly, of endeavouring to ascertain definitely, in a small area and on a small scale, what animals habitually lived in, and what animals descended to, the mid-water strata (matters of very great importance from the standpoint of oceanic distribution).

I venture to submit that, as long as the Law of Gravity holds good, the absolute closure of my net is indisputable, for it is effected by gravity.   It is not only certain in the actions of opening and shutting (gravity being here also the motive power), but, when shut, the net-frame closes so tightly that nothing larger than the net-mesh (1 mm. or 75 mm.) can get into it, either going down or coming up.

This being so, my observations agree on general lines with those of Chun and the 'National,' and directly contradict the purely negative observations of the 'Blake' and 'Albatross' on which Agassiz bases his theory of an Azoic zone.   I encountered animals at every depth down to 500 fathoms, the deepest water available.

The Faeroe Channel was indicated as a suitable district by the thermal conditions ; the depth is small when compared with the great oceans, but the extremely low temperatures met with in the district are those of the greatest depths in open oceans.   As regards every thing but pressure, which appears to be an unimportant factor in determining distribution, the conditions of life at 500 fathoms in the " cold area " of the Faeroe Channel seem to be those of the greatest midwater depths known [1].

The Faeroe Channel is certainly a " closed sea " in the technical

[1] The Faeroe Channel was further indicated by the fact that H.M.S. 'Research' was surveying in the Orkney district.   I cannot sufficiently express my obligations for the assistance rendered to me on so many sides—the recommendation of the Council of the Royal Society, the assent of the Lords Commissioners of the Admiralty, the suggestions of Admiral Sir William Wharton and Captain Tizard of the Hydrographic Office, and the uniformly patient help of Captain Moore and the other Officers of the 'Research' in both years

sense of the word ; but it is not a closed sea like the Mediterranean or Gulf of California, in which high temperatures are maintained to such a depth that there is practically no thermal limit to the descent of a surface organism.   It is a closed sea on one side only, open to the Arctic Ocean on the North-east, with the isothermobath of 35° F. at about 250 fathoms, and in many places with a temperature of 30° F. at 500 fathoms.   One is far from land nowhere in the Faeroe Channel , the single station of 1897 (Sta. 20) being only about a hundred miles from Cape Wrath, but far enough to be beyond the range of continental influence, in a case where the continental slope (100 to 500 fathoms) is steep, and no rivers discharge into the sea.   The water at these depths is directly derived from the open Arctic ocean, and is practically unaffected by continental influence.

I would urge therefore, as against Prof. Agassiz, that planktonic animals can and do flourish at greater depths than 200 fathoms, even under oceanic and not neritic conditions : that they apparently flourish in utter darkness, at a temperature of 30° to 32° F., and at a depth of at least 300 to 400 fathoms

The animals captured in the mid-water appear to fall into at least five categories :—(1) Organisms which range indifferently over all depths (eurybathic); of these, at any rate so far as the Faeroe Channel is concerned, *Calanus finmarchicus* may be taken as an example (p. 544 *ante*) · (2) those which live habitually at great depths, and rarely or never appear at the surface, if at all, generally at night ; of these characteristically mesoplanktonic animals, the Tuscarorida of the 'Challenger' Expedition, the deep-sea Schizopoda of Prof. Chun, *Sagitta whartoni* and *Conchœcia maxima* of the 'Research' collections[1] may be cited : (3) those which spend their earlier life at or near the surface, but of which adults are almost or quite confined to deep water, such as *Nyctiphanes norvegica* : (4) those which when adult inhabit the surface, but spend their larval life at considerable depths, such as Chun's Ctenophora (5) the corpses of any of the foregoing classes, and of purely epiplanktonic animals, such as *Temora longicornis* (p. 546, table, *ante*).

With regard to this latter class, it will no doubt be urged by some naturalists that the capture of organisms in the Mesoplankton points, not necessarily to the fact of their living at great depths, but to their having been killed at the surface by unfavourable physical conditions and their subsequently sinking through the deeper strata towards the bottom.   In many cases this is no doubt the true explanation of their presence in deep water : I have suggested this as the explanation of a particular haul of *Doliolum* (p. 583 *infra*), and of the presence of six species of Copepoda (pp. 548-9, *supra*) in the 'Research' collections from the Mesoplankton.

(1) In cases where *numerous* observations on *successive* days in the *same* district show numerous specimens of a species in the upper strata, but only a few specimens are rarely, not constantly, taken in the lower zones, this explanation probably holds good, especially in a Frontier district (p. 545) such as the Faeroe

[1] Proc. Zool. Soc. 1896, p 992 ; 1897, p. 523.

Channel, where hotter and colder surface currents are constantly at war.

(2) This explanation may probably be further extended to cases such as those of the six Copepoda already mentioned (pp. 548-9); they appear to be southern (warm-water) forms, driven by the North Atlantic Drift into higher latitudes (colder temperatures) than they can bear. Although southern forms, none of them were taken at the surface in 17 hauls, five were captured once and one twice in 13 Mesoplankton hauls; all six were few in numbers.

(3) A different explanation seems reasonable in the case of species which are taken in numbers and with regularity at considerable depths, but appear rarely or never at the surface (if at all, then generally at night) It is to me inconceivable that the destruction of such a small surface population should produce dead specimens in such abundance and with such regularity in the deeper strata *Euchœta norvegica*, *Metridia longa*, and *Pleuromma abdominale* (pp 543 and 547) are examples of this distribution, they seem to be forms which, at any rate in these latitudes, exhibit a preference for a mesoplanktonic existence, but which can and do exist at the surface also under certain circumstances. Two of the species are Arctic type-forms, which in these latitudes seek deeper (colder) water, and may perhaps eventually be taken very much further south as Mesoplankton than they have as yet been recorded in surface collections.

(4) When a species is taken in equal abundance and with equal regularity both in Mesoplankton and Epiplankton, it seems fair to infer that it is eurythermal and eurybathic; it does not seem possible that all the deeper specimens are deep merely because they are dead and sinking. For example, the list of the captures of *Calanus finmarchicus* on the 'Research' (p. 542) seems to exclude such a possibility.

It seemed worth while to cite these instances of criteria, which may be applied in dealing with collections of Plankton from various zones, if the observations are numerous enough and sufficiently near together in time and place to permit of any general conclusions at all being drawn. Most mesoplanktonic specimens are dead when they arrive inboard; the sudden alterations of pressure and temperature, and the damage by the net itself, are most fatal; further, decay is so retarded at low temperatures in sea-water, that not even microscopical examination can be relied on as evidence of the life or death of the organism at the moment of capture. The criteria applied above may be expressed thus:—

Specimens at surface	Specimens below	Species belongs to
Numerous, constant	None, or occasionally a few.	Epiplankton.
Numerous, constant	Numerous, constant.	Epiplankton and Mesoplankton.
None, or occasionally a few.	Numerous, constant.	Mesoplankton.

The table on pp. 542-3 showing the vertical distribution of the
'Research' Copepoda in the Faeroe Channel, seems to me to offer
convincing proof of the existence of a living Mesoplankton. If
the forms which I caught at great depths were all dead, there
would be more dead species in the district than live ones, which
seems absurd; the average number of species per haul is ·88 in
the Epiplankton and 1·38 in the Mesoplankton. Further, the deep
water would contain an abundance of dead specimens of a species,
such as *Euchæta norvegica*, of which there were practically no
specimens at the surface to be killed, which also seems absurd.
Again, if the destruction at the surface is so extensive as the death-
hypothesis would imply, some specimens at least of *Temora longicornis*, and of all such forms as are abundant at the surface, ought
to be captured in the lower strata; yet this species was not once
taken in the Mesoplankton.

In concluding this discussion of the general question, I would
strongly urge that any attempt, seriously to investigate the Mesoplankton in future, should be made, not at random stations all over
the ocean, but in a limited area, one which presents as far as possible uniform conditions throughout, and may be presumed to
contain a similar fauna throughout; for only by *numerous successive
hauls at all depths* can that careful comparison be made, which will
enable the observer to assign to each organism the proper significance of its occurrences.

Doliolum (Dolioletta Borgert[1]) tritonis, Herdm. = *D. denticulatum* Herdman[2]

This species presented no new anatomical features for record.
As Herdman points out[2], some specimens are cylindrical rather
than of the characteristic barrel-shape; he assigns this to imperfect
preservation A comparison of my specimens from different
stations with specimens of other animals from those stations, leads
me to believe that the alteration in shape is due to damage in the
tow-net by pressure. The smallest sexual specimens which still
carried the stalk of attachment to the "Pflegethier" were about
5 mm, it had been lost in one of 7 mm. length.

The horizontal distribution of this species was enormously extended by the 'National' (Plankton Expedition); till 1889 it had,
I believe, only been taken in the Faeroe Channel, the North Sea,
and off the Hebrides; the 'National' captured it in that year over
nearly the whole of their course, from the Labrador Current right
down to the South Equatorial Drift.

The appearance of huge swarms of sexual forms of *D. tritonis*

[1] A. Borgert, Thaliacea der Plankton Expedition.—C. Vertheilung der
Doliolen 1894
[2] W A Herdman Trans Roy Soc Edinburgh, xxxii p. 101.

in the Faeroe Channel is very perplexing. On the second and last days out of eight in 1896, they were at or near the surface in enormous quantities (96 to 140 specimens in a haul of 10 to 15 minutes); on the other six days, they were not only scarce or absent at the surface, but could not be found even by the deep-water net. Our position was altered several times between the two days of their swarming. This seems to imply that D. *tritonis* occurs in patches, with a few outliers in between the patches. Similar swarms of this species were observed in the Faeroe Channel by the 'Triton' in 1882 [1], by the 'Holsatia' in 1885, by the 'National' in 1889.

Brandt [2], in an interesting discussion of swarms such as these, seems to incline to the view that they are produced by wind and current action; but it is a little difficult to imagine how the effect of these agents would gather scattered organisms into a broad swarm in the open sea, except in an eddy or backwater; although they might make "wind-rows" in the open sea, or swarms in a closed area such as the Mediterranean. Further, if wind and current were the main direct agents in collecting swarms of D *tritonis*, other organisms of the same powers of locomotion ought also to swarm at the same time; this is not my experience, nor, so far as I know, have other observers recorded this as a feature of the case.

I should prefer for the present to regard a swarm of D *tritonis* mainly as the result of a period of great reproductive activity. In the case of an organism with a rapid power of multiplication and definite reproductive periods (whether due to food, temperature, or other causes), a very large number of individuals will soon be produced nearly simultaneously, if they have but little power of self-locomotion, *as long as they lie in the track of fairly uniform wind and current*, such as the North Atlantic Drift ("Gulf Stream"), *there seems to be no reason why they should be parted one from another* In an eddy, such as the Sargasso Sea, where there are no constant winds or constant currents, the tendency will probably be for every little shift of wind to part them The swarms of various organisms met by the 'National' were apparently all in the track of great ocean-currents, and were conspicuously absent from the Sargasso Sea.

If my suggestion is correct, then in still or steadily moving water a few *Doliolum* "Ammen," fairly close together, will produce a crop of "Pflegethiere" by asexual generation more numerous than themselves, and although we do not know the rate of reproduction of the "Amme" in throwing off "Pflegethiere," still that each "Pflegethier" may throw off an enormous number of sexual forms is obvious from the hundreds of buds on the stolon of each Pflegethier. The rate of reproduction is extremely *rapid*; and I see no reason to believe that in a constant current the family would not move forwards as a whole.

[1] " At times the Doliolum appeared to be in vast banks, where they were very numerous, between these banks there were always a few stragglers " (Murray in Herdman, *op cit* p 112)

[2] Brandt in Reisebeschreibung der Plankton Expedition, p 356 (1892)

It would appear also that the reproduction (throwing off) of sexual forms is *periodic*, from the following facts :—

The 'Research' specimens consisted of very numerous fully-grown sexual forms, a few much smaller sexual forms, and a few large 'Pflegethiere." Other observers[1] have recorded much the same for the same time of year (July, August).

Taking this in conjunction with the fact that, in my collections at any rate, sexual specimens of intermediate size, between the less than 5 mm. and the more than 9 mm. specimens, were very scarce, it would appear that the swarms were due to a period of simultaneous throwing off of numerous sexual forms; their existence and growth being, naturally, only possible when, as Borgert suggests, the conditions of food, temperature, &c. are favourable.

The above remarks apply to the 'Research' collections of 1896. In 1897 we were able to collect on one day only. On this occasion *Doliolum* was rare at the surface (like everything else). and the bulk of the catch was at a considerable depth. The small specimens were, proportionately to the large, very much more numerous at the surface than in the collections of 1896; the larger forms seemed to have sunk, like almost everything else, under the influence of very cold and somewhat boisterous weather The following table gives the numbers taken .—

Sta	Haul in fathoms.	Temperature.	Specimens.
20 e	0		16 large[2], 4 small
20 f.	0		4 ,, 0 ,,
20 g	40 to 0		1 ,, 25 ,,
20 a	200 to 100		0 ,, 0 ,,
20 b.	300 to 200		11 ,, 0 ,,
20 c	400 to 300		3 ,, 0 ,,
20 d	500 to 400		130 ,, 9 ,,

As they were almost absent from the Mesoplankton during the 1896 cruise, I should not like to suggest, without more extended observations, that the deeper specimens were at so great a depth and so low a temperature, of their own free will. It seems to me probable, although there was nothing in their appearance either to suggest or to contradict it, that, in the haul 20 d, the net struck a swarm which had been killed by cold or other unfavourable circumstances, and was slowly settling to the bottom. The only differences between the specimens from 20 c and 20 d, and those surface-specimens which were living when brought on board, was that the digestive coil was blue in the deep-water specimens, brown or reddish in the surface specimens. Experiment would easily determine whether this was a post-mortem change or not.

[1] "Such vast numbers . .. with a very few exceptions of much the same size" (no Pflegethiere noticed), Herdman, *op cit* p. 111 —"Erst bei genauerer Durchsicht fand ich unter ihnen, wenn gleich in weitaus geringerer Zahl, Pflegethiere und auch Ammen"; Borgert, *op cit.* p 61. "Ammen" were not observed among the 'Research' specimens
[2] Three were "Pflegethiere"

On the Occurrence of *Doliolum nationalis* (Borgert) in
British Waters.

By the courtesy of Mr. E. T. Browne and of Mr. E. J. Allen,
the Director of the Plymouth Laboratory, I have been able to
examine specimens of the alleged *Doliolum tritonis* from Valentia
and Plymouth. These southern specimens prove to be *D. nationalis*
Borgert[1]; they differ from *D. tritonis* not only in their much
smaller size, but in the point of origin and attachment of the
branchial lamella.   A further difference between the species, not
discussed by Borgert, is shown by the relations of the intestine :
in *D. tritonis* (correctly figured by Herdman[2]) this is short, thick,
and sharply curved on itself,   in *D. nationalis* (correctly figured
by Borgert, pl. v. fig. 4) it is long and slender, and, after a nearly
straight course posteriorly, it is only slightly curved forwards,
often not so much so as he has figured.

D. nationalis appears to be a southern and warm-water form.
It has only been described hitherto from the collections of the
'National' (German Plankton Expedition) in 1889 : it was absent
until the 'National' struck the true Gulf Stream (37° N. 59° W.,
surface temperature 79° Fahr.); from there it occurred with
greater or less regularity through the Sargasso Sea, North
Equatorial, Counter Equatorial ("Guinea Current"), and South
Equatorial Drifts, right up to the mouth of the English Channel
(49° 7' N., 5° 8' W., surface temperature 52° Fahr.), where one
specimen only was captured   It appears to be only an occasional
visitor to our shores, probably under the influence of prevalent
south-westerly winds and warm weather; it occurred at Plymouth
and Valentia in 1893[3] and 1895[4].

Parathemisto abyssorum (Boeck).

This species according to Hansen[5] and Sars[6] is probably identical
with *Hyperia oblivia* Kroyer; a view now accepted by Bovallius[7].
H. oblivia Spence Bate, appears to be not identical with either of
the above.

Its distribution vertically and horizontally is a little perplexing,
so far as our information goes at present

i. It lives in cold water, apparently at the surface, in Greenland
seas (Kroyer[8] and Hansen[5]), and in the Murmanske Hav, North
of Russian Lapland (Hansen[9]).

ii. It lives in cold water at great depths—from 1710 to 160

---

[1] *Op cit.* p. 581 *supra.*
[2] *Op cit.* p 581 *supra*, pl xx fig 1.
[3] W Garstang Journ. Mar Biol. Assoc. iii. p. 222. See also p. 210 for an account of the weather that year.
[4] E T Browne. Journ Mar Biol Assoc iv. p 171
[5] Hansen Malacostraca marina Grœnlandiæ occidentalis.
[6] G O Sars Crustacea of Norway, vol 1 p 11
[7] Bovallius Kongl Svenska Vetenskaps-Akad Hdlg xxi. p 251
[8] Kroyer. "Gronlands Amfipoder," Vidensk Selsk , nat -math Afh.vii p.229.
[9] Hansen: Dijmphna Togtets zool.-bot. Udbytte, 1886, Krebsdyr, p 28.

fathoms at 6 stations of the Norske Nordhavs Expedition [1]; all along the West Coast of Norway up to Finmark from 100 to 200 fathoms (Sars [2]), in the cold area of the Faeroe Channel (H.M.S. 'Research,' 1896, 530 to 220 fath).

iii. It appears to come up to the surface from great depths at night, in the Faeroe Channel (H.M.S 'Research,' 1896, Station 15 d), it has been taken off the Shetlands [3], and in the Faeroe Channel by the 'Triton' in 1882

iv. It has been recorded from shallow waters round our coasts . from Banff (Edwards [4]). from the Forth [5], once, a single specimen, from the Clyde (Robertson) [6]; off St. Andrews (McIntosh) ; from Valentia, where what appeared to be very young specimens of this species were taken in profusion by Messrs. A. O. Walker and E. T. Browne. Mr. Walker also informs me that he has received specimens 5 mm in length from off Galley Head, co. Cork.

Now the curious fact about the specimens from Valentia, Galley Head, and the Firth of Forth is that they are all very small, ranging from 2 to 5 mm.; whereas in the Faeroe Channel they are mostly about 7–10 mm. in length, and specimens from the Norwegian North Atlantic Expedition reached the length of 17 mm. The length of the Banff specimens is not given. In all probability the small size of the British specimens of this sub-Arctic form indicates either (1) that the species attains a smaller size under increased temperature ; or (2) that the larger adults are oceanic, and come inshore to breed, dying or retreating again to the open sea afterwards (this is Mr. Walker's suggestion), or (3) that the small and apparently young specimens of our coasts normally live in the open sea but nearer the surface than the adults, and are only driven on to our shores in heavy weather, or by a southerly current.

I have nothing to adduce either for or against the first suggestion. Against Mr. Walker's suggestion, it may be urged that the adult forms have not been recorded from inshore waters, and would surely have been noticed if they arrived in great numbers to breed. For, one feature of the appearance of this species on our coasts is that it generally arrives in enormous numbers (Firth of Forth, Banff, Valentia in 1896, they were less numerous, but plentiful at Valentia in 1897): this would imply the presence at some time of numerous parents, which have never been recorded.

The third suggestion appears to me to be likely to prove the correct solution: namely, that both young and adults normally inhabit open water, the young living nearer the surface and being brought to our shores as occasional visitors under special circumstances of weather and current. The clue is to be found in an

---

[1] G O Sars Norske Nordhavs Expedition, Crustacea, vol. ii. p. 37.

[2] G. O Sars Crustacea of Norway, vol. i p. 11.

[3] A M. Norman Rep British Association for 1868, p. 287.

[4] Edwards Journ Linn Soc ix. p 166

[5] Sir John Murray kindly sent me a sample of these.

[6] Robertson Trans N H Soc. Glasgow, n s ii p 69 (1890).

Tribe THALASSINIDEA.

Family CALLIANASSIDÆ.

Genus CALLIANIDEA H. M.-Edwards, 1837

29. CALLIANIDEA TYPA H. M.-Edwards, 1837.

Callianidea typa, H. M.-Edwards, H. N. Crust. ii. p. 329, pl. xxv. bis, figs. 8–14 (1837).

From Rotuma six specimens; from Funafuti six specimens.

EXPLANATION OF THE PLATES

PLATE LXIII.

Fig 1 *Metapenæus commensalis*, n. sp., p. 1001, side view. × 1½.
1 a   „   „   head from above. × 2
1 b.   „   „   3rd maxilliped
2 a *Stenopus hispidus* (Olivier), p 1002, 1st abdom append. of ♀
2 b   „   „   1st abdom append of ♂.
3 *Caradina vitiensis*, n sp, p 1003, side view. × 4.
3 a   „   „   head from above
4. *Periclimenes danæ* (Stimpson), p 1004, side view   × 8
4 a   „   „ head from above. × 10.
4 b.   „   „ 3rd maxilliped
5. *Periclimenes rotumanus*, Borradaile, p 1005, side view. × 5
5 a.   „   „ head from above. × 5.
5 b.   „   „ 3rd maxilliped.

PLATE LXIV.

Fig 6. *Periclimenes vitiensis*, Borradaile, p 1005, side view. × 3
6 a.   „   „ head from above. × 3
6 b   „   „ 3rd maxilliped
7. *Coralliocaris brevirostris*, Borradaile, p 1006, side view. × 4.
7 a.   „   „ head from above   × 4
7 b   „   „ 3rd maxilliped.
7 c   „   „ chela of 2nd pair
7 d.   „   „ dactyle of 3rd leg
8 *Palæmonella tridentata*, n sp., p. 1007, side view. × 4.
8 a.   „   „ head from above   × 4
8 b.   „   „ 2nd maxilliped.
8 c   „   „ mandible

PLATE LXV

Fig 9 *Athanas sulcatipes*, n sp, p 1011, ♂, side view   × 8
9 a   „   „ head from above × 8.
9 b.   „   „ 3rd maxilliped
9 c.   „   „ 2nd maxilliped.
9 d.   „   „ 1st maxilliped
9 e   „   „ 2nd maxilla.
9 f.   „   „ 1st maxilla
9 g   „   „ mandible
9 h.   „   „ 1st antenna
9 i.   „   „ smaller leg of 1st pair of ♀.
10 *Alpheus funafutensis*, n sp, p. 1013, side view. × 4.
10 a   „   „ head from above × 4.
10 b.   „   „ 3rd maxilliped.
10 c   „   „ 2nd maxilliped.
10 d.   „   „ 1st maxilliped.
10 e.   „   „ 2nd maxilla
10 f.   „   „ 1st maxilla
10 g.   „   „ mandible.
10 h.   „   „ smaller leg of first pair.

6. Contributions to our Knowledge of the Plankton of the Faeroe Channel[1].—No. VII. A. General Data of the Stations. B. The Protozoa. C. The Medusæ By G. HERBERT FOWLER, B.A., Ph.D., Assistant Professor of Zoology, University College, London.

[Received December 6, 1898.]

(Plate LXVI.)

A —GENERAL DATA OF THE STATIONS.

In the table now exhibited (see p. 1019) will be found the chief details of the successive collecting stations of H.M.S. 'Research' in the Faeroe Channel, 1896 and 1897· Stations 11[2] to 18 being in the "Cold Area," between July 30 and Aug. 6, 1896; Station 19 in the "Warm Area," Aug. 7, 1896; Station 20 in the "Cold Area," July 7, 1897.

The physical conditions of the Channel have been fully dealt with in the Reports of the various exploring expeditions[3] which have surveyed this classic district, of which it is not an exaggeration to say that the very beginnings of modern oceanography were made in its somewhat troubled waters.

DETERMINATION OF THE HORIZONS.

The horizons through which the Mesoplankton net remained open in 1896 were thus determined. In the first place, experimental hauls were made near the surface, to determine the number of fathoms through which the net must be towed at an approximately constant speed in order that the propeller (1) might open the net, (2) might shut it again. Of these experimental hauls, the contents of which were mostly not kept, the last one retained was 12 d.

[1] Owing to the scanty leisure at my disposal, the series of papers under this title has been unavoidably disconnected.

The first three numbers dealt with some conspicuous and interesting species, the fourth, by Mr I. C Thompson, with the Copepoda, the fifth, by Mr E. W L Holt, with the fish-larvæ, the sixth furnished a description of the special nets used for the Mesoplankton, and a short discussion of the general question of a midwater fauna. This and the future papers will discuss the organisms captured, group by group, and show their horizons by tables when necessary.

The references to previous papers of the series in the Society's Proceedings are ·—No I, 1896, p 991, No. II, 1897, p. 523, No III, 1897, p. 803; No IV, 1898, p. 540, No. V, 1898, p 550, No VI, 1898, p 567

[2] Stations 1-10 were collecting-grounds in the neighbourhood of Kirkwall and do not concern the 'Research' cruises.

[3] C. Wyville Thomson 'Depths of the Sea' London, 1873, 8vo (H.M S 'Lightning' and 'Porcupine').—T. H. Tizard and J. Murray "Exploration of the Faeroe Channel in 1880." Proc Roy. Soc. Edinb xi. p. 638 (H.M hired ship 'Knight Errant').—T H Tizard "Soundings and Temperatures obtained in the Faeroe Channel during the Summer of 1882 " Proc. Roy. Soc. xxxv. p. 202 (H.M.S 'Triton ').

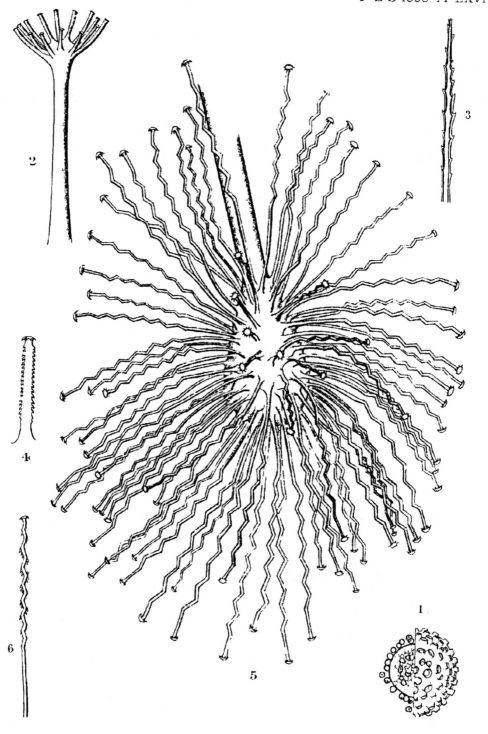

The procedure was then as follows :—The net and machinery, weighted up to 100 lbs., were lowered overboard, and a number of fathoms run out, slightly greater than that of the sounding in the case of the lowest horizon ; the angle made by the line when taut was approximately measured, and a calculation made from Traverse Tables in the ordinary way as to the depth which the net had reached. As I have pointed out already [1], this, the usual method, is most fallacious ; for the towing-line does not form the hypotenuse of a right-angled triangle (as presupposed by this method), but an unknown catenary, which is practically uncalculable except

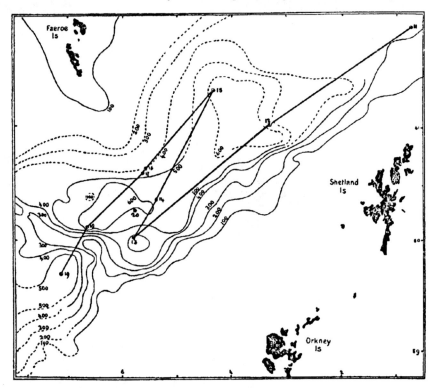

CHART OF THE FAEROE CHANNEL,

Showing the collecting-stations of H M S. 'Research' in 1896 and 1897. The contour-lines have been roughly plotted from the Admiralty Chart and from the soundings taken on these cruises. they are dotted where the soundings are far apart (Station 20 (1897) is N of Station 13)

by tedious experiment in order to obtain the necessary data. The fallaciousness of this method was brought home to me by striking bottom at 398 fathoms (Station 16 a i) with 450 fathoms of warp out, though by quadrant and traverse tables the net should only have reached 300 fathoms. Fortunately all the details of the previous hauls had been kept ; and as there was sufficient evidence, from

[1] Proc Zool Soc. 1898, p 568.

the condition of the paint and the small quantity of bottom-deposit
in the collecting-tin, that the net had not more than touched
bottom without dragging on it, I was able to get, from this
accident, data for the correction of the other deep-water hauls.
While, therefore, the horizons of the Mesoplankton hauls may
perhaps be understated (if the net had rested long on the bottom
in haul 16 *a* 1), the depth is certainly not exaggerated.

That the calculation of the depth reached in this manner was
a very close approximation to the truth, can fortunately be shown
in another way. During the 1896 cruise, Captain Moore and the
other Officers were engaged in taking serial temperatures[1]; and a
minimum thermometer was sent down on the locking-gear of my
net with every haul after 12 *e*. A comparison of the temperatures
thus recorded on the net, and of the temperatures independently
observed or interpolated on a curve by the Officers, is given
below, where column I. shows the station number and haul letter,
column II., the probable depth reached by the net (about 50
fathoms below the point at which it opened) as calculated from the
data furnished by Station 16 *a* i when the net struck bottom; column
III., the temperature recorded by the thermometer on the net, after
correction; column IV., the temperatures for the depth given in
column II., as independently observed or interpolated in the curves
in Captain Moore's Report.

I.	II.	III.	IV.	
13 *a*	180	47 0	47·0	
13 *b*	356	32·6	33·0	
13 *d*	445	32·0	31·25	
13 *e*	445	32·0	31 25	
13 *g*	516	30·75	31 0	
15 *c*	578	31 0	30·75	
16 *a* i	400	30 6	30·9	at 380 fath.
16 *a* ii	356	31·0	31·5	
18 *b*	578	31 0	31·0	at 600 fath
19 *a*	534	46·0	46·8	at 550 fath

Considering the different times of day, and the slightly different
positions owing to the ship's drift, at which the two sets of observations were made, their approximation is very close.

With the net of the 1897 pattern, which presented less resistant
surface and less buoyancy than the other, no calculation of the
depth was required: the line hanging vertically to the surface, the
number of fathoms paid out indicated the depth sufficiently
accurately. As to the rate of travel of the messengers, had time
(i e weather) permitted, this would have been carefully worked into
a curve as it was, the impact could be felt at the less depths, and
had to be guessed (good margin being allowed) for the greater
depths. That the messengers travelled very rapidly was shown
by the deep dints that they received on striking the locking-gear.

[1] W. U. Moore· Reports of Proceedings in connection with Investigations
into the Physical Conditions of the Water of the Faeroe Channel.—Hydrographic Department. Admiralty, 1896, 4to.

TEMPERATURES.

The temperatures given in the table are compiled from the readings of the thermometer on my net, and from the observations and interpolations published by Captain Moore (*op. cit. supra*).

Station Number and Haul Letter.	Position of ship.	Sounding in fathoms.	Horizon explored, in fathoms.	Temperature (Fahrenheit) of horizon explored.	Meshes per inch
11 *a* .	61° N., 0° long	203	100–±0	48°–54°	25
11 *b* ..	,,	,,	0	54°	180
11 *c* .	,,	,,	30–0	49°–54°	36
12 *a* ...	61° N , 3° W.	502	±350–±150	31°–43°	25
12 *b* ..	,,	,,	10–0	53°	36
12 *c* ..	,,	,,	0	53°	180
12 *d* .	,,	,,	130–±0	44°–53°	25
12 *e* .	,,	,,	450–320	30°–32°	25
12 *f*	,,	,,	?10–0	? 53°	9 36
13 *ab* .	60° N , 5° W	575	300–0	33°–54°	25
13 *c* .	,,	,,	2–0	54°	36
13 *d* ...	,,	,,	400–270	32°–38°	25
13 *e* .	,,	,,	400–?	32°–?	25
13 *f* .	,,	,,	0	54°	180
13 *g* .	,,	,,	558	465–335	31°–33°	25
13 *h*	,,	,,	0	54°	180
13 *i* ..	,,	,,	100–0	48°–54°	36
13 *k* ..	,,	,	624	2–0	53°	36
13 *l* .	,,	,,	0	53°	180
14 .	,,	,,	—	0	54°	180
15 *a* .	61° N , 4° W	610	2–0	53°	36
15 *b* .	,,	,,	0	53°	36
15 *c* .	,,	,,	530–0	31°–53°	25
15 *d* .	,,	,,	0	53°	13
16 *a* i .	60° N , 5° W	398	350–220	31°–37°	25
16 *a* ii	,,	,,	300–170	33°–44°	25
16 *b* .	,,	,,	0	53°	36
16 *c* .	,,	,,	4–0	53°	36
17 .	,,	,,	—	0	53°	13
18 *a* ...	60° N , 6° W.	645	3–0	53°	36
18 *b*	,,	,,	530–400	31°–?32°	25
19 *a* .	59° N , 7° W	595	480–350	46°–47°	25
19 *b*	,,	,,	480–0	46°–54°	25
19 *c* .	,,	,,	4–0	54°	36
19 *d* .	,,	,,	10–0	54°	36
20 *a* .	60° N., 5° W.	560	200–100	39°–46°	40
20 *b*	,,	,,	300–200	33°–39°	40
20 *c* .	,,	,,	400–300	31°–33°	40
20 *d* .	,,	,,	500–400	30°–31°	40
20 *e* .	,,	,,	0	52°	36
20 *f* .	,,	,,	0	52°	180
20 *g* .	,,	,,	40–0	52°	36

CLASSIFICATION OF THE HAULS.

In the first table (p. 1019) the hauls are arranged in succession of number and letter, in order to facilitate reference ; but in the subsequent tables of species they will be classified as Epiplankton (0 to $+100$ fathoms), Mesoplankton ($+100$ fathoms from surface to $+100$ fathoms from bottom); and "doubtful hauls," in which the net failed to shut at the expected horizon, or in which the contents of two hauls were accidentally mixed. On comparing these tables of species with that given in Mr. Thompson's paper on the Copepoda[1], it will be found that a few changes have been made. No. 12 a has been moved from among the "doubtful" to the Mesoplankton hauls, because it certainly closed somewhere near 100 fathoms, although perhaps not so low as 150 ; 12 f proves, by the character and condition of its contents, to have been made very near the surface, and has been put with the Epiplankton hauls ; 13 e, about which I entered a note of suspicion in the station-book when it arrived inboard, proves to contain several essentially epiplanktonic organisms which do not occur in any other Mesoplankton haul, and has therefore been relegated to the "doubtful" category : in all probability one of the chains hung on the trigger for some time after the net should have completely closed ; the details of this haul will be given later.

B.—THE PROTOZOA.

It was not to be expected that this group would yield much information with regard to the special object of the cruise, the Mesoplankton fauna. For the efficient study of the Protozoa, the nets must be extremely fine, so fine that they must be towed very slowly ; and if they are towed slowly, a large part of the other constituents of the catch will escape. Special hauls with special nets, or a special arrangement inside the large mesoplankton net (which I hope to try shortly), are requisite for successful captures. On the other hand, some of my hauls show that certain Phæodaria live at great depths, although they do not show that any species are confined to the Mesoplankton.

As regards the surface Protozoa, no special attempt was made to collect them, for they were not required for comparison with the Mesoplankton fauna ; and, further, my finest net, the only one suitable for Protozoa, was almost entirely devoted in 1896 to the capture by Dr. Stericker, R.N., of vegetable plankton for the Scottish Fishery Board A few new and interesting forms of considerable size were, however, obtained.

Two things are apparent on a glance at the table of Protozoa— the one, the epiplanktonic character of the three Peripylaria ; the other, the way in which several species are aggregated in the same haul, while other hauls show few or no Radiolaria. They seem to

[1] Proc Zool. Soc 1898, pp 542-3

appear and disappear together in accordance with varying external conditions.

Only those species appear in the table, the horizons of which seem to be in any way significant; the horizons of the rest will be simply recorded in the text

RADIOLARIA PERIPYLARIA.

THALASSICOLLA sp.

A number of specimens of this genus, taken chiefly at the surface, could not be assigned with certainty to any species already described. As with *Collozoum*, observations on living material seem to be necessary in order to determine the specific position. The following characters are enumerated here in order to assist future recorders in identifying the form from this locality:—The striated calymma is very thick and colourless, the alveolar layer internal to this is also very thick and colourless, with large alveoli; the extracapsular pigment is generally yellowish, occasionally dark in colour, the central capsule is dark and considerably thicker than in *T. nucleata*; in specimens of which sections were made, the membrane of the central capsule appeared to be divided up into numerous small polygonal areæ, with a single large pore in the centre of nearly every area, the nucleus is circular, with a thickish nuclear membrane and irregular nucleolus, intracapsular inclusions?

The proportion of central capsule to nucleus, often utilized as a specific character, does not appear to be trustworthy for this purpose. The table below gives this proportion in a number of specimens, apparently all referable to the same species: column I. shows the total diameter in millimetres, arranged in order of size, column II. shows the diameter of the central capsule expressed as a percentage of the total diameter.

I.	II.	I.	II.
3 38	29	1 27	38
3·29	19	1·26	33
2·10	40	1·23	28
1·96	21	1 11	33
1·96	21	1·09	32
1·90	30	1·09	32
1·75	22	1·07	21
1·70	22	·93	37
1·68	41	·92	30
1·61	21	·77	26
1·47	23	·63	36
1·44	22		

The proportions of striated calymma, alveolar layer, and central capsule showed similar variations.

It seems highly probable from the table that this *Thalassicolla* is

	Station Number and Haul Letter	Horizon in fathoms	*Thalassicolla* sp.	*Collozoum* sp.	*Siphonosphaera tizardi*, sp. n	*Aulacantha lævissima* Hkl	*Aulographis* sp.	*Aulographus moorensis*, sp. n.	*Auloceros trigeminus* Hkl.
Epiplankton.	11 a	100–±0	···			·	·	·	··
	11 b	0	+	+	+				
	11 c	30–0	+	+	··			···	··
	12 b	10–0				···		···	··
	12 c	0	··					···	
	12 d	150–±0							
	12 f	? 10–0	·	·	···			···	··
	13 c	2–0	··	+	··			···	
	13 d	0		···				···	
	13 h.	0			+				
	13 i.	100–0	+	+	++	+	·	···	
	13 k.	2–0	+	+	++	··		···	···
	13 l	0		+					
	14.	0		+		·	··	··	···
	15 a	2–0				··			···
	15 b.	0		,					
	15 d.	0							
	16 b	0	+	+			··		··
	16 c.	4–0	+	+			·	·	
	17	0	+				··		
	18 a	3–0	+	+	+		··		·
	19 c.	4–0	··	·	+		··		
	19 d.	10–0	···	·	··		···		
	20 e	0		··	··		·		
	20 f.	0		··	··	···		··	
	20 g.	40–0	·	··	··	··	··		
Mesoplankton.	12 a.	±350–±150	·		···	···	·		
	12 e.	450–320							
	13 d.	400–270							
	13 g	465–335	+	··	··	+	···	···	+
	16 a i.	350–220							
	16 a ii	300–170	··	·	··				···
	18 b	530–400	···	·		·	·	·	···
	19 a	480–350	··	·	·	+	+	+	+
	20 a	200–100	·	··	·	···			···
	20 b	300–200	···	·	·	·			
	20 c.	400–300	·	·	·				
	20 d	500–400	+	·	·				
Doubtful.	13 a b	300–0	+	+	··	+	·	·	+
	13 e	400–?	+	+	+	·	··		+
	15 c.	530–0	·		+	··	+		
	19 b	480–0	··	+	+	+	·	··	

Aulocoryne zetesios, gen et sp. n.	Aulosphaera flexuosa Hkl.	Calodendrum ramosissimum Hkl	Coeloplegma murrayanum Hkl.	Lizzia blondina Forbes	Sarsa spp.	Solmaris sp	Solmundella sp	Aglantha ? rosea Forbes	Aglantha ? digitalis O.F.M	Trachynema sp
...	.					+				
..	..		+	+	+		...	+		
...	...	.	...	++	+					
...	.	.	.	...	+					
...			+	+		++				
...	+	+	+	.		++		+		
..	...		+	..		++				
..	.	...				+				
..	..	...	...	+	+		..	?		
...	..	..	.	+	+	++				
..	..	.	+	..	.	++	+	+		
..			.	++	+	+++				
...	..			+	..	+++				
...				+	...	+				
.	...		..	..	.	.		..	+	
?	+	..	+							
...		.		.		...		...	+++	
...		..	+	...		...	+	..	+++	+
.	..	..		...		..	.		+++	
.	...		..	.		+		..	+++	
	...	..				...			+	
...	+	.	+	..		+		..	+	+
?	+	.	+			+	+	...		
...	...	.	+	.					...	+

an epiplanktonic form; it was plentiful at the surface, but in 13*g*
and 20*d* only single specimens were captured, which were probably
dead or dying and sinking to the bottom.

For the horizons of capture, see the table on p. 1022.

COLLOZOUM spp.

Of this genus there were apparently two separate species
represented in my collections, neither of which could be attributed
to *Collozoum inerme* from the warm Atlantic, or to *C ellipsoides*,
described by Haeckel from the Faeroe Channel.   In the one type
the largest spherical zooids of the colony measured about ·05 to
·07 mm. in diameter, in the second type about 09 to ·16 mm.;
both had about ·2 to ·28 mm. of calymma and alveoli outside the
zooids.   In the first type there was a considerable thickness of
alveolar calymma in the centre of the colony, as in the ordinary
C. inerme; but in the spherical or lenticular colony of the second type
the zooids were so closely aggregated in the centre of the colony
as all but to touch one another, and were surrounded by a thick
alveolar layer and a thick radiately striate calymma, exactly as a
Thalassicolla.

Although I have no doubt that at least one undescribed species
of *Collozoum* occurs in these waters, I do not feel justified in
naming and describing it without a detailed examination of living
material.

Both types were confined to the Epiplankton, except for a few
specimens in haul 13 *e*, which appears to have remained open
through higher horizons than was intended or at first believed,
and is now included with the doubtful hauls.   As the *Collozoum*
occurred in 30°/₀ of the Epiplankton hauls, and in no undoubted
Mesoplankton haul, I think we are justified in regarding it as
essentially epiplanktonic.

For the horizons of capture, see the table on p. 1022.

LAMPOXANTHIUM MURRAYANUM, sp. n.[1]

Definition of the Species.—Spicules of the skeleton numerous,
geminate-radiate, with a short axial rod, from each of which
spring three or four acute shanks, devoid of branches or forks
(sometimes three shanks at one end, four at the other).   Both rod
and shanks smooth and straight; shanks two to three times the
length of the rod   Calymma full of large alveoli.   Diameter of
calymma 3·5 mm.; diameter of central capsule 1 mm.

This large and beautiful species is undoubtedly referable to
Haeckel's genus *Lampoxanthium*, but I am unable to place it with
certainty in any of his subgenera, and it agrees with none of his
species.   In addition to the geminate-radiate spicules there are

[1] I have great pleasure in dedicating this species to Sir John Murray.
K C B , F R S , who is specially associated with the Faeroe Channel by his part
in the exploration of the district in the 'Knight Errant' (1880) and 'Triton'
(1882).

also a few which may be radiate, or may be only broken off from the end of a geminate-radiate spicule.

The horizon of capture was doubtful; one specimen was taken at 13 *e*, one at 13 *ab*.

SIPHONOSPHÆRA (HOLOSIPHONIA) TIZARDI, sp. n.[1] (Plate LXVI. fig 1.)

Definition of the Species.—Colony spherical (? always), up to about 2 mm. diameter. Zooids with a single spherical lattice-shell about ·15 mm. in diameter, which is beset all over by short broad tubes. The tubes are very thin-walled and fragile, their walls slightly convergent, ·010 to ·018 mm. in diameter, and about ·005 mm. high; there are five to seven tubes on the half meridian. Endosarc with very numerous nuclei; oil-globules?; zooxanthellæ very numerous, both inside and outside the shell, and also scattered through the calymma between the zooids.

In some hauls large numbers of the zooids had apparently broken away from the calymma, and appeared as solitary organisms referable to the family Liosphærida. As a warning to describers of Liosphærida, I may say that I had actually identified them as *Ethmosphæra leptosiphonia*, described by Haeckel from the Faeroe Channel, before I found them united in a colony.

So far as the evidence goes, the species is purely epiplanktonic; as it is a very conspicuous form, and it occurs with fair regularity at the surface (23 % of epiplankton hauls), and never with certainty in mesoplankton hauls, I think we are justified in accepting the evidence as fairly conclusive.

For the horizons of capture, see the table on p. 1022.

RADIOLARIA ACANTHARIA.

Acanthometron catervatum Haeckel (=*A. brevispina* Hkl.) was present in most hauls with the fine-meshed net in 1896, often in sufficient quantity to give a red tinge to the contents of the tow-net. In 1897 (Station 20) it was practically absent from the surface, like most things. A similar abundance and scarcity were recorded by the 'Knight Errant' in 1880 in this district[2].

RADIOLARIA PHÆODARIA.

This interesting group of Radiolaria was well represented in the 'Research' collections, but not so well as in the 'Triton' collections made by Sir John Murray in 1882.

The data afforded by my captures show the extreme danger of drawing conclusions as to the vertical distribution of a species from a few observations at a single "station." I have already pointed out[3] that adequate data for this work can only be obtained

---

[1] I have pleasure in associating with this species the name of Captain T. H Tizard, R N., who explored the Faeroe Channel in command of the 'Knight Errant' (1880) and of H.M.S 'Triton' (1882), to whom I am indebted for much valuable help

[2] T. N Tizard and J. Murray, Proc. Roy. Soc. Edinburgh, xi. p 654.

[3] Proc Zool Soc. 1898, pp. 578-580.

by numerous observations at all depths on successive days in a small area, and even these cannot be safely applied to a species unless it occurs *constantly and in fair number in a large percentage of the hauls* The table of Phæodarian captures given on pp. 1022-3 would seem at first sight to point to about 100 fathoms as the upper limit of all the species except *Cœloplegma murrayanum*; but the weakness of such an inference would lie in the fact that none of them were captured with anything like regularity in the Meso-plankton. That the argument would be false is shown by the fact that two of them were taken by Sir John Murray at the surface from H.M.S. ' Triton ' in the same waters.

All the conclusions that can be drawn for the Faeroe Channel, from so few observations as those in the table, are :—

(1) That *Cœloplegma murrayanum* is both epiplanktonic and mesoplanktonic, extending to at least 350 fathoms (19 a) and a temperature of 33° Fahr. (13 g). The large number of specimens taken at 13 g and 19 a, and the small number taken at or near the surface, showed that the deep specimens were not merely dead and sinking to the bottom.

(2) That *Aulacantha lævissima* and *Aulosphæra flexuosa* may occur at considerable depths in the Mesoplankton; since the ' Triton' results showed them to exist at the surface also, they are, like *Cœloplegma murrayanum*, to be regarded as epiplanktonic and mesoplanktonic. Though not present in such numbers as the first species, they were plentiful enough to make it extremely improbable that the specimens were dead and sinking

(3) That *Aulographis moorensis* and *Auloceros trigeminus*, var , occur in the Mesoplankton, but it does not appear whether they are confined to it or not.

AULACANTHA LÆVISSIMA Haeckel. (Plate LXVI. fig 3.)

The youngest specimens referable to this genus in the 'Research' collections agreed entirely with Haeckel's description of *A. lævissima*, except for the presence of a few extremely minute teeth on the larger spines. Larger specimens, however, with a central capsule about ·4 mm. in diameter, and spines at least ·9 mm. in length and calymma about 2 mm. in total diameter, exhibited a distinct denticulation (Plate LXVI. fig. 3). As *A. lævissima* has been described only from the Faeroe Channel, it is probable that my specimens belong to the same species as those of Haeckel. I have therefore retained the name for " the smoothest " species described up to the present.

For the horizons of capture, see the table on p. 1022.

AULOGRAPHIS (AULOGRAPHONIUM) MOORENSIS[1], sp. n. (Plate LXVI. figs. 2, 4.)

Definition of the Species.—Radial tubes rounded proximately,

[1] With this new species I am glad to associate the name of Captain W. Usborne Moore, R N , of H M.S. ' Research,' to whose help I owe no small part of such success as my midwater experiments attained.

equally broad for most of their length, but then tapering slightly towards the distal end, at which the tube expands suddenly into a broad circular cushion.   The margin of this cushion bears two verticils of radially divergent, slightly curved, terminal branches, about 10 to 16 in number; these are about twice as long as the inflated end of the tube is broad.   Each branch is armed with two lateral rows of numerous recurved denticles, and bears a terminal spathilla of 5 to 8 recurved teeth (Plate LXVI. fig. 4).

One specimen . 480–350 fathoms, 46°–47° Fahr. (Station 19 *a*).

AULOCEROS (AULOCERÆA) TRIGEMINUS Haeckel, Var. nov.

A few shattered specimens, of what is probably only a variety of the species above named, exhibited a verticil formed by the twice-repeated dichotomous branching of the radial tubes, each verticil thus consisting of eight tynes.

The type species is known only from the 'Challenger' Station 353, between St. Vincent and the Azores, at a probable depth of 2965 fathoms (open tow-nets).

For the horizons of capture, see the table on p 1022.

AULOCORYNE ZETESIOS [1], gen. et sp. n.   (Plate LXVI. figs. 5, 6).

Aulocoryne (Family Aulacanthida) .—Radial tubes without lateral branches, terminating in a club-shaped expansion which carries numerous fine radiating spines.

Aulocoryne zetesios ·—The spines of the terminal club are thin, tubular, at first straight or slightly curved, then regularly zigzag, lastly straight, they are finely denticulate, and terminate in a spathilla of about 8–10 recurved teeth (Plate LXVI. fig. 6).

A single specimen only of this species was captured.   Although so broken that not a single head was left on the radial tubes, many heads had been fairly well preserved with the calymma, and there could be no doubt as to its structure.   The fine spines of the terminal club are of the same character as the tangential spines of *Cannorhaphis spathillata* and the radial spines of *Cœlodrymus anchoratus*: the same types of growth recur again and again in the various families of Phæodaria, first as scattered spicules, then as tubes radiating from the central capsule, then bound together in a coherent skeleton.

Unfortunately, the exact record of the horizon was lost; it was captured in either 13 *e* or 13 *g*.

CŒLODENDRUM (CŒLODENDRIDIUM) RAMOSISSIMUM Haeckel.

This species was fairly plentiful at Station 13 *i*.   It has been described as cosmopolitan. from various stations and depths, but not, I think, from so far north as the Faeroe Channel.

CŒLOPLEGMA MURRAYANUM-TRITONIS Haeckel.

These species of Haeckel are the extremes of a series of very

---

[1] αὐλός, κορύνη, tubular club, ζήτησις, in honour of H M S 'Research.'

varying forms, all terms of which were represented in the 'Research' collections. The range in depth is now extended to 480–350 fathoms; the lowest temperature to 31°–33° F. It has not been recorded except from the Faeroe Channel.

For the horizons of capture, see the table on pp. 1022–3.

FORAMINIFERA.

GLOBIGERINA spp.

1. A very small species, probably a dwarfed *Gl. bulloides*, was fairly plentiful whenever the finest net was used at the surface. The specimens were spinous when captured [1].

2. On the occasion when the Mesoplankton net touched bottom, a very small quantity of bottom deposit was found in it, containing minute spineless Globigerinæ, which seemed to be referable to the species *G. bulloides* and *G. pachyderma*. It is very noticeable in balsam mounts of this sample that most of the supposed *G. pachyderma* are quite filled with what looks like brownish protoplasm, as are most of the bottom-living Foraminifera, but that most of the thin-shelled *G. bulloides* are clear and empty.—The brownish material, while yellowing slightly with nitric acid, does not give the brilliant tint of the usual xanthoproteic reaction. It would seem to be of a clayey nature, and is possibly, as Sir John Murray suggests, a stage in the formation of glauconite. It is extremely soft and friable, and when stained is almost indistinguishable from the similarly stained protoplasm of surface specimens.

The dependence of the formation of glauconite upon the presence of protoplasm has been pointed out in detail by Sir John Murray and the Abbé Renaud (Chall. Rep., Deep-Sea Deposits, pp. 385–390). If this material be of a glauconitic nature, its method of occurrence would seem to indicate that *G. pachyderma* on reaching the bottom contains more protoplasm than *G. bulloides*, and in that case probably lives nearer to the bottom. It is very desirable that voluminous samples of the bottom deposit should be taken in the Faeroe Channel in order to test this suggestion, and for the following reason.

The whole discussion as to whether *Globigerina* was a purely planktonic form, or could both float and creep at the bottom indifferently, would probably have been settled by the acceptance of the first alternative years ago, had it not been for an observation by Dr. Carpenter during the third cruise of the 'Porcupine' [2] which was recorded in his general discussion of the *Globigerina* question in 1875. This was to the effect that samples of water taken from immediately above the *Globigerina* ooze at 500–750 fathoms, in the Faeroe Channel, yielded on filtration "multitudes of young *Globigerinæ*," plentiful and small enough to make the water appear turbid.

The "cold area" of the Faeroe Channel is apparently the

[1] *Cf.* Brady Proc. Roy. Soc. Edinburgh, xi. p. 717.
[2] W. B. Carpenter Proc. Roy. Soc. xxiii. p. 235.

southernmost limit[1] for the occurrence of *G. pachyderma* in bottom deposits ; it is abundant in Arctic deposits, but has never been recorded alive from the surface. *G bulloides*, on the other hand, is only known to occur at the surface, although dead shells are plentiful in the deposits of the Faeroe Channel.

I venture to suggest that Dr Carpenter's observation as to the presence of very small living *Globigerinæ* just above the bottom may be harmonized with the generally accepted view that most, if not all, *Globigerinæ* are essentially planktonic organisms, by the supposition that *G. pachyderma* is a mesoplanktonic form, at any rate in the Faeroe Channel. It is quite possible that it may occur at the surface farther north, but it would escape capture by any but the finest nets (diameter of the shell ·3 mm., according to Brady ; my largest specimens were about ·15 to 2 mm.).

SILICOFLAGELLATA.

DICTYOCHA sp.

A fair number of spicules referable to this genus of Ehrenberg occurred in one or two surface-hauls, notably 13 *h*. They agreed on the whole with the spicules of *D. stapedia* and *rhombus* (Haeckel), but no sign of the protoplasmic body was traceable. Prof. Cleve[2] records *D fibula* and *D. speculum* (Ehrenberg) for the same cruise.

DINOFLAGELLATA.

In reporting on the vegetable Plankton of the cruise of the 'Research' in 1896, Prof Cleve[3] records the following species of Dinoflagellata :—

Ceratium tripos Duj.
Ceratium furca Duj.
Ceratium tripos Ehrenb. ; var. *baltica* Schutt ; var. *macroceros* Ehrenb. = var. *scotica* Schutt ; var. *longipes* Bail. = var. *tergestina* Schutt, var. *horrida* Cleve.
Peridinium divergens Ehrenb.
Pyrophacus horologium Stein.
With the exception of the last, with which I did not meet, all these occur in all hauls with the finest net, many of them in great abundance.

CILIATA—OLIGOTRICHA.

DICTYOCYSTA ELEGANS Ehrenberg.

A beautiful species of this genus was fairly plentiful in some hauls, notably 13 *h*. According to Moebius[4] all the various forms of *Dictyocysta* are referable to Ehrenberg's species *elegans*, an

[1] H B Brady. Chall. Rep Zool , ix Foraminifera, p 600 (*cf.* pp xii–xiv).
[2] 'Fifteenth Annual Report of Fishery Board for Scotland,' part iii p 302.
[3] P. T. Cleve: Fifteenth Annual Report of Fishery Board for Scotland, 1896, part iii p. 297
[4] O Moebius Funfter Jahresbericht d Commission z. wiss. Untersuch d. deutschen Meere, 1887

opinion which, I think, is not likely to be accepted by the next monographer of the group. My own specimens agreed exactly with Moebius's figure 28, pl. viii., and showed no signs of variation in the direction of other species. As regards the structure of the shell, I can confirm von Daday [1] as against previous observers in the belief that the neck (Aufsatz) consists of a meshwork, but that the body of the shell (Wohnfach), although appearing at first sight to be also a meshwork, is really a closed chamber. My specimens seem to show that the inner membrane of the " Wohnfach " is continuous everywhere except at the mouth, but that the outer membrane ceases at the so-called pores.

C.—THE MEDUSÆ.

My friend Mr. E. T. Browne has been kind enough to look over the few Medusæ of my collections. Of all groups this seems to suffer most in capture at sea. Near shore, or from an open boat, in fairly still water, the tow-net can be handled delicately, but on board ship in open water the characteristic sense-organs and delicate tentacles are broken by pressure against the tow-net, whether in the rolling of the ship or in the hauling of a meso-plankton net by steam-power from considerable depths.

In 1897 I tried to lessen the damage to surface forms, both by diminishing the net-mouth in proportion to the surface-area of the net, and by attaching the net-warp to a single-strap ' accumulator' of india-rubber; these certainly diminished, but did not avoid, damage. Only in a few cases was Mr. Browne able to assign a specific name; his list is as follows :—

1 *Lizzia blondina* Forbes
2 *Phialidium* sp
3. *Sarsia* sp.
4 *Sarsia gemmipara* Forbes
5 *Solmaris* (possibly) two spp.
6 *Solmundella* sp
7 *Aglantha rosea* Forbes
8 *Aglantha digitalis* Haeckel
9 *Trachynema* sp

Of these the first five are probably purely epiplanktonic. *Lizzia blondina* was often present in such numbers as to tinge the contents of the tow-net.

Phialidium sp. (14) and *Sarsia* spp. (several hauls) presented no special features.

Solmaris sp. is almost certainly confined to the Epiplankton. A single specimen occurred in 20 c (400–300 fathoms); but as it occurred in 53 % of Epiplankton hauls, often in great profusion, and only a single specimen in one Mesoplankton haul, the presumption is that the latter specimen was dead and sinking to the bottom [2]

As to *Solmundella*, my captures do not afford any evidence of its vertical distribution.

[1] E von Daday Mittheil zool. Station in Neapel, vii p. 486.
[2] Compare Proc Zool Soc 1898, p 579

What appeared to be broken specimens of *Aglantha rosea* of Forbes occurred in small numbers in three surface hauls.

The eighth species,

AGLANTHA DIGITALIS (O. F. Muller, Haeckel pars),

represents such of Haeckel's *A. digitalis* as remains after the restoration of Forbes's *A. rosea*, and the removal of *A. digitalis* var. *occidentalis* Maas[1]. In his great monograph Haeckel[2] put Forbes's *A. rosea* with eight marginal vesicles, and the old *A. digitalis* of O. F. Muller and Fabricius with four marginal vesicles, under the single species *A. digitalis*. Since then both species have been confused, until again separated by Browne[3]. It is consequently at present impossible to detail accurately the distribution of these two species, but it seems to be certain that *A. digitalis* occurs off Greenland and Northern Norway, and that *A. rosea* occurs as a neritic form round the British coasts (Valentia, Shetland, Heligoland). The one is certainly an Arctic form, the other a southern, even though they may overlap to a greater extent than we at present know.

This being so, it is not without significance that Mr. Browne, when going over my specimens without knowing the horizons, separated the *Aglanthœ* into two groups, *A. rosea* and *A. digitalis*, of which, on comparison with the station list, all the *A. rosea* were found to come from surface hauls, all the *A. digitalis* from deep hauls[4]. As *A. digitalis* was captured in 66°/₀ of Mesoplankton hauls, and never at the surface, the presumption is that it has, like other Arctic surface forms, sunk to deeper strata on reaching lower latitudes (warmer surface water).

Unfortunately the results of the 'National' do not throw any further light on the distribution of these two species, horizontally and vertically, for Maas (*op. cit. supra*) accepted Haeckel's fusion.

TRACHYNEMA sp.

A few specimens of a large medusa were apparently referable to this genus. Hemispherical in shape (15 mm. diam., 12 mm. high), its eight radii showed the heavy transverse musculature of *Trachymedusæ*. The eight tentacles were stumpy and thick, one at the end of each radial canal. The sense-organs had disappeared. The manubrium was about 5 mm. long, devoid of a "Magenstiel," and provided with four very small oral lappets. What seemed to be rudiments of generative organs were placed on the upper third of the radial canals.

[1] O Maas: Ergebnisse d. Plankton-Expedition Die craspedote Medusen, p 24

[2] E Haeckel System der Medusen, 1 p. 272

[3] E T. Browne. Proc. Zool Soc 1897, p 833

[4] One small specimen of *Aglantha*, too much damaged for reference to either species, was taken at 16 *b* In the table it has been placed as a query under *A. rosea*

It is the only *Trachynema* which approaches *T. funerarium* Hkl. in size; but its proportions, and the position of the generative organs, are against its being a young form of this species. In most recognizable points it lies between *T. octonarium* Hkl. and *T. eurygaster* Hkl.; but it agrees exactly with neither. The eight radial canals and manubrium were of a strong brick-red.

It occurred in deep or doubtful hauls only.

EXPLANATION OF PLATE LXVI.

Fig 1. *Siphonosphæra tizardi*, sp n , p 1025   A single individual is represented by half the shell and by half a section of the central capsule outside the latter are zooxanthellæ   Cam luc

Fig 2   *Aulographis moorensis*, sp. n , p. 1026.   Termination of a radial tube. Cam luc

Fig 3   *Aulacantha lævissima* Haeckel, p 1026.   Termination of a radial tube in optical section, showing the denticulations   Cam luc

Fig. 4. *Aulographis moorensis*, sp n., p 1026.   A single terminal branch of a radial tube, showing the denticulations and spathilla   Cam. luc

Fig 5.   *Aulocoryne zetesios*, gen et sp. n , p 1027   Termination of a radial tube, showing the club covered with zigzag spines.   This beautiful drawing is due to the skill of Miss Mabel Green

Fig. 6. *Aulocoryne zetesios*, gen. et sp n , p. 1027   A single zigzag spine. Cam. luc.

8. Contributions to our Knowledge of the Plankton of the Faeroe Channel.—No. VIII.[1] By G. HERBERT FOWLER, B.A., Ph.D., F.Z.S.

[Received December 20, 1902.]

(Text-figures 13–17.)

The present paper contains notes (in some cases due to the valued help of friends) on *Beroe, Arachnactis, Podon*, the Ostracoda, the Copepoda, the Amphipoda, and the Schizopoda, captured by H.M.S. 'Research' in 1896 and 1897 in the Faeroe Channel.

CTENOPHORA.

BEROE CUCUMIS Fabricius.

This species, characteristic of cold Arctic currents [2], was taken in the following hauls :—

16 *a* ii , 300 to 170 fathoms, seven specimens.

13 *e*, 400 to ? fathoms, one fragment.

20 *d*, 500 to 400 fathoms, one specimen.

Most specimens showed the characteristic brick-red or rose tint, and though much battered and in some cases inverted, were referable with a fair amount of certainty to this species.

ANTHOZOA.

ARACHNACTIS ALBIDA M Sars.

Some information as to the developmental succession of the mesenteries in this form was given in No. III. of this series. Since its publication, I am glad to say that it has been substantially corroborated by Prof. van Beneden [3].

He agrees with my suggestion to separate the Channel and North Sea *Arachnactis* from *albida* of the Faeroe Channel, and describes it under the name of *lloydii*, under the idea, which is probable, but at present unproved, that it will be shown eventually to be the larva of *Cereanthus lloydii*. Till this has been proved, I venture to think it better to retain my provisional name of *bournei* for this form.

The occurrences of *A. albida* are shown in the table (p. 118): it occurred in over 61 per cent. of epiplankton hauls, never in a mesoplankton haul, and may fairly be taken to be a purely epiplankton form It was present in considerable quantity, as many as 50 specimens having been taken in one haul.

[1] The references to previous papers in the Society's Proceedings are :—No I , 1896, p 991, No. II , 1897, p 523 ; No III , 1897 p. 803, No IV , 1898, p 510, No V , 1898, p 550, No VI , 1898, p. 567, No VII , 1898, p 1016 I regret that various circumstances, mostly beyond my control, have caused so great a lapse of time between this paper and No VII

[2] Chun 'Die Ctenophoren der Plankton-Expedition,' p 26

[3] Van Beneden 'Anthozoaires de la Plankton-Expédition.'

	Station Number and Haul Letter	Horizon in fathoms.	Beroë cucumis Fabr.	Arachnactis albida M Sars	Podon intermedius Lilljeborg	Conchoecia marina Br. & Norm	Calanus finmarchicus Gunner.
Epiplankton.	11 a.	100–±0	.		.		+
	11 b.	0		+			++
	11 c.	30–0		++			+++
	12 b	10–0			+		+++
	12 c.	0	...	+	++	...	+++
	12 d.	130–±0		++	..	...	++
	12 f.	?10–0	.	++	..	...	..
	13 c	2–0		++	++		
	13 f	0		++	+		
	13 h	0					
	13 i	100–0		++	++	.	+
	13 k.	2–0		++	++	...	..
	13 l.	0					
	14	0		.		..	+
	15 a.	2–0				..	+
	15 b.	0		+		...	+
	15 d	0			...	..	+
	16 b.	0				..	+
	16 c.	4–0		+			+
	17.	0					
	18 a.	3–0		++	+	...	+
	19 c	4–0	...	++	.	...	++
	19 d	10–0	.	++	..	...	..
	20 e	0		++			
	20 f.	0		++	.	.	
	20 g.	40–0		..	.	..	+
Mesoplankton.	12 a.	±350–±150		.	.	..	..
	12 e.	450–320			.		+
	13 d.	400–270			.		+
	13 g.	465–335				+	+
	16 a i	350–220				+	+
	16 a ii	300–170	+				+
	18 b	530–400					+
	19 a	480–350				+	++
	20 a.	200–100				+	++
	20 b.	300–200					+
	20 c.	400–300				+	++
	20 d.	500–400	+	.	+	+	++
Doubtful.	13 a b.	300–0		+	..	+	++
	13 e	400–?	+	+		+	++
	15 c.	530–0				+	++
	19 b.	480–0	+			.	++

Eucalanus attenuatus Dana. Cf. note p. 123	Euchaeta norvegica Boeck.	Metridia longa Lubbock.	Pleuromma abdominale Lubbock Cf. n p. 123.	Acartia clausi Giesbrecht	Temora longicornis Muller.	Thysan. longicaudata, adult.	Thysan. longicaudata, larvæ & sublarvæ.	Nyctiphanes norvegica M. Sars.	Thysanopoda microphth. Ortmann	Parathemisto oblivia Kroyer.
..	+	+		+	+	.	+			
+	+	+ .	.	+	++	...	+++			
+	+	+	.	+	.	..	+	+		
+		+			.	+ +	+			
			.	+	++		+			
		.	...		.	+ +	+			+
..	..	.		+	+	..	+			
+	.	.	...	+	+	+	+			
	.	.		++	..	+	+			
+	+	+	.			+	+		.	+
+	+	+	+			+.	+			+++
+	+	+	+	.		++		+	+	+++
	+	+	+			++				+
+	+	+	+	+.	.	++				
.		+	+	+						
		++	+	+		++		+	+	+
+	+	++				++				
++	++	+				++		+	+	+

PHYLLOPODA.

PODON INTERMEDIUS Lilljeborg

My friend the Rev. T. R. R. Stebbing, F.R S., was kind enough to identify and count the specimens of this species. It would no doubt have occurred in more of the surface hauls had not my finest tow-net been devoted to the collection of Diatoms for the Scottish Fishery Board. It is no doubt a purely epiplanktonic form in the Faeroe Channel, a single specimen only was taken at 20 d (500–400 fathoms) as against about 106 specimens in 7 hauls at the surface ; the single deep specimen was probably a sinking corpse.

This species is, I believe, known only from the surface [1]; it ranges over the Baltic, Norwegian coast up to Vadso, Denmark, Boulogne, Concarneau, Trieste.

OSTRACODA.

The representatives of this order belonged exclusively to the Halocypridæ, and were mostly taken in the mesoplankton. Only one species, *Conchœcia maxima*, occurred sufficiently often to allow of a generalization as to its horizon

The identification of a Halocyprid is rarely satisfactory without dissection of the mouth-parts, which means destruction of the specimen. I have, however, dissected a considerable number, and feel at all doubtful only in the case of *C. porrecta* ; I have preferred, however, to leave the specimens under this species rather than create a new species on the strength of slight differences in the armature of the mandible.

The table following shows those surface and deep-water hauls, made by Professor Chun between Finistère and the Canary Islands with open vertical nets [2], which contained the same species as

Haul.	Horizon in fathoms.	*Conchœcia hyalophyllum.*	*Conchœcia porrecta*	*Paraconchœcia oblonga*	*Halocypria globosa*	*Conchœcilla daphnoides*
II.	546 to 0	.	*	.		
III.	819 to 0	...	*	*	Various depths	*
IV.	546 to 0	*	*	*		*
VII.	873 to 0	. .	*			..
	Surface.			*	*	..

[1] J de Guerne : Bull Soc Zool. France, xii 341 (1887)   W. Lilljeborg 'Cladocera Sueciæ,' Upsala, 1900, 4to

[2] Chun SB kon preuss Akad Wissensch. (1889 xxx   Claus 'Die Halocypriden,' Wien, 1891, 4to.

were captured by the 'Research' in the Faeroe Channel; they are cited in the text by Roman numerals.

CONCHŒCIA MAXIMA Brady & Norman.

As I have previously pointed out[1], this species appears to be purely mesoplanktonic, in the latitude at any rate of the Faeroe Channel. It occurred in 50 per cent. of the mesoplankton hauls, and in three hauls which began at or over 300 fathoms and finished at the surface; it was not captured once in hauls between 100 fathoms and the surface (cf. table, p. 118). The species was fairly common.

The record of previous captures was cited in the second paper of this series[1], and also indicated a mesoplanktonic habit in subarctic regions, but it is not surprising that in yet colder waters it should appear at the surface. At 84° 32' N., 76° E, it was captured with a surface-net by the 'Fram'[2], and is recorded as abundant in most of the samples of Crustacea from this voyage[3].

CONCHŒCIA HYALOPHYLLUM Claus.

Twelve specimens in haul 13 i, 100 fathoms to surface Five specimens too small for satisfactory identification, but perhaps referable to this species, occurred in hauls 20 c and 20 d

Claus[4] records as other occurrences Chun's haul IV , Ischia at 492 fathoms, Orotava at the surface.

? CONCHŒCIA PORRECTA Claus.

Numerous specimens from 20 a b c d and one from 13 i. Claus (op. cit.) records it from Chun's hauls II., III., IV., VII.

CONCHŒCIA BOREALIS G. O. Sars.

A single specimen in haul 19 a, 480 to 350 fathoms. Recorded previously from 250 to 300 fathoms at the Lofoten Islands[5], and from Trondhjem Fjord at 150 fathoms[6]. This appears to be a purely cold-water form.

PARACONCHŒCIA OBLONGA Claus.

Six specimens in haul 20 c, four in 20 d. Claus (op. cit. p. 64) cites this species as from Chun's hauls III. and IV.; and states that it also occurs at the surface, but without giving authority or details. He remarks on the probable identity of this species with G. W Muller's variabilis[7], a suggestion with which Muller seems to agree[8]. This would extend the distribution considerably, as Muller[7] records it, from the 'Vettor Pisani' collections of

[1] Proc. Zool Soc 1897, p 523
[2] F Nansen · Norwegian North Polar Expedition. G. O. Sars: Crustacea, p. 11.
[3] Id ibid p 137
[4] C Claus, op cit p 61
[5] G O Sars · Forh Vid -Selsk. Christiania (1865), vol 1866, p. 120
[6] G. S Brady & A M Norman Trans Roy Dublin Soc (2) v p 686.
[7] G W Muller "Ueber Halocypriden," Zool Jahrb Syst v. p. 273.
[8] G. W. Muller . 'Ostracoden des Golfes von Neapel,' p 229.

Chierchia, as occurring at various points in the tropics at depths between 382 and 546 fathoms; it occurs also in the Gulf of Naples. Brady[1] records it as having been taken by the 'Challenger' Expedition off Kandavu, Fiji, and between Marion and Crozet Islands at unrecorded depths.

Halocypria globosa Claus.

Six specimens in haul 13 *i*.

This species is known from the surface and at various depths in the Atlantic[2], and is recorded from Gibraltar as taken by the 'Vettor Pisani'[3]. Of specimens taken by the 'Challenger,' the record was in one instance lost[4]; other specimens were captured at the surface between Api and Cape York[5]. It seems to be a form widely distributed both vertically and horizontally.

Conchœcilla daphnoides Claus.

Only three complete specimens, and one empty carapace, referable to this genus were obtained. The specimens on which Claus founded the genus (with this single species) were all young males: larger specimens of the genus, including females, were obtained by Sir John Murray on H.M.S. 'Triton' in 1882, from the Cold Area of the Faeroe Channel, and were described by Canon Norman and Dr. Brady under the specific name of *lacerta*, not without the "suspicion that they may perhaps belong to the adult form of *C. daphnoides*"[6]. My own specimens were too few to settle the point, but as the two smaller specimens most resembled in outline the figure of Claus, and the two largest that of Brady and Norman, I have left them provisionally under the older specific name.

In addition to Chun's hauls III. and IV., it has been captured at 200 fathoms off Achill Head (*daphnoides*), the Faeroe Channel as above (*lacerta*), and off Kandavu, Fiji, at an unrecorded depth[7] (*daphnoides*).

Copepoda.

Mr. I. C. Thompson was kind enough to report on the Copepoda in No. IV. of this series of papers[8]. Since that date, the arrangement of three then doubtful hauls has required modification: 12 *a*, which was suspected at the time of capture to have remained open too long, proves to have no apparent contamination of undoubted surface forms, and has been moved to the Mesoplankton, 13 *e* was also suspected, in this case with justice, as

[1] G. S. Brady. "Myodocopa of the 'Challenger' Expedition," Trans Zool. Soc. xiv p. 95.
[2] C Claus, *op. cit.* p 79
[3] G. W. Müller. Zool Jahrb. Syst v. p 270.
[4] G. S. Brady & A. M. Norman: Trans Roy. Dublin Soc (2) v p. 705
[5] G S Brady Trans Zool. Soc. xiv. p. 97.
[6] G S Brady & A M Norman Trans Roy. Dublin Soc (2) v p 697.
[7] G S Brady Trans Zool Soc. xiv p 95.
[8] Proc. Zool. Soc. 1898, p. 540.

containing several undoubtedly epiplanktonic species (e. g. *Arachnactis albida*), and has been relegated to the "doubtful" category, closure of the net not having taken place at the proper time; 12*f* was known to be epiplanktonic, although there was some doubt as to the exact depth at which it had been towed. I have therefore reprinted in the table (pp 118, 119) the captures of the seven forms which were taken at least six times, sufficiently often to give approximate data for an estimate of their vertical distribution In discussing this question, I gave a short table on p. 546 showing the occurrences of these seven species expressed in percentages of those Epiplankton and Mesoplankton hauls which contained Copepoda; this can now be amended as follows, omitting the four doubtful hauls from the calculation :—

	Epiplankton.		Mesoplankton.
	Total hauls containing Copepoda.		
Calanus finmarchicus occurred in	83 %	and in	91 %
[1] *Eucalanus attenuatus* „	22 „	„	41 „
Euchæta norvegica „	11 „	„	75 „
Metridia longa „	22 „	„	75 „
[1] *Pleuromma abdominale* „	5 „	„	58 „
Acartia clausii „	33 „	„	25 „
Temora longicornis „	33 „	„	0 „

The amended table is in harmony with the conclusions drawn from the former, as to the vertical distribution of these forms, except in the case of *Acartia clausii*, the question of which was expressly reserved (*op. cit.* p. 549).

Since the publication of Mr. Thompson's report, I found that Dr R. Norris Wolfenden was making an exhaustive study of the fauna of the Faeroe Channel, and naturally placed my collection at his disposal. He has been kind enough to furnish the following notes on new and other species, with some of which he has already dealt briefly elsewhere [2]. Exact data of depth &c. were not always available, as by the time that Dr. Wolfenden received the specimens all the epiplankton hauls of a station had in many cases been put together in one bottle, all the mesoplankton hauls in another, for economy of space.

PLEUROMMA ROBUSTUM Dahl, Zool. Anzeig. v. p. 16 (1893).

"This is the common *Pleuromma* of the Faeroe Channel, and was found to be present in considerable numbers in Dr. Fowler's collection, *Pl. abdominale* occurring much more rarely. In these northern latitudes it almost entirely replaces the latter species. It is readily distinguishable by the horseshoe-shaped mass of red pigment which is present in the anterior and inferior portion of the head at the base of the mouth-organs, and in the male by

---

[1] Dr. Wolfenden points out that as, according to his wide experience, *Eucalanus attenuatus* is nowhere met with in the Faeroe Channel, unless perhaps quite exceptionally, these figures probably refer to *Eucalanus elongatus* Similarly, for the species *Pleuromma abdominale* should probably be substituted *Pl. robustum*.

[2] R N. Wolfenden Journ Marine Biol Assoc. (1902), vi p. 344.

the clasping antenna being on the left side, and the pigment-spot invariably on the right side. The second feet in both male and female have the characteristic notch and hook on both limbs. Length 3–4 mm. Haul 20 *a* (200 to 100 fms) and several others."

HETEROCHÆTA ZETESIOS ♂ , Wolfenden, *op cit* p 367.

"The head is like *H papilligera* Gbt   Though the end joints of both anterior antennæ were broken off, the 19 joints left had a length of over 4 mm , with the geniculation between the 18th and 19th segments. The anterior antennæ were therefore much longer than the whole animal, which was 3·5 mm. There was considerable asymmetry of the furcal segments, that on the left being much the longest and broadest. The anterior foot-jaw had one thick hooked bristle on the 5th lobe, but no "tooth-comb" bristle, and the 5th feet were peculiar and unlike those of any other *Heterochæta*, displaying an upright and stiff process of the 2nd basal joint, armed with fine stiff hairs on the inner aspect (like a " tooth-comb "), and the proximal inner margin of the 1st joint of the exopodite with a protuberance armed with 4 teeth. The 2nd basal joint of the foot of the opposite side is armed distally with short stiff bristles. It could be only the male of *H. grimaldii* or of *H. longicornis*, neither of which is yet known, or of *H. major* (Dahl). The latter and *H grimaldii* are very large (5–10 mm.), and though *H zetesios* resembles *H. longicornis* in some points, it is perhaps better for the present to distinguish it as a new species. Only one example was met with in Dr. Fowler's collection, in haul 20 *a* (200 to 100 fathoms)."

ÆGISTHUS ATLANTICUS Wolfenden, *op. cit.* p. 364.

" The occurrence of an example of this genus in the Faeroe Channel is remarkable. This specimen was found in the collection made by Dr Fowler as 20 *a* (200 to 100 fathoms)   It had a total length of 1·45 mm., a 6-segmented anterior antenna with very long and peculiar sensory processes. It has distinct differences from *Æg. mucronatus* or *Æg. aculeatus* Gbt , and also from the species described by Scott from the Gulf of Guinea as *Ægisthus longirostris.*"

LUCICUTIA MAGNA Wolfenden, sp n. ♂

" A single specimen found in Dr. Fowler's collection from 19 *a* (480 to 350 fathoms), of 3·54 mm. length, was apparently new. The anterior antennæ were larger than the whole body, by the terminal one and a half joints   The endopodite of the 1st foot was two-jointed. The right 5th foot has a strong spiny process on the inner side of the 2nd basal and the exopodite of two segments ; the endopodite and exopodite of the left 5th foot being each of three segments. The size alone distinguishes it from the males of any other known species, only *L grandis* being larger."

AUGAPTILUS ZETESIOS Wolfenden, *op. cit.* p. 369.

"One specimen only was found, in the bottle marked 19 *a. c.* Another specimen occurred in the sample marked 20."

EUCALANUS CRASSUS Gbt. 1888, Atti Acc. Linc., and 1892, Fauna u. Flora Neapel, v. p. 19.

"This species was of not infrequent occurrence, especially in the bottles marked B 1 and 13 *k* (2 to 0) and 13 *i* (100 to 0).

"The writer also has frequently noted its occurrence in the Facroe Channel."

GAETANUS MAJOR Wolfenden, sp. n.

"Two examples of this genus (*Gaetanus*) were found in Dr. Fowler's collection marked 19 *a* (480 to 350 fathoms). The copepod very greatly resembled *Gaetanus armiger* Gbt., but the anterior antennæ were longer, reaching beyond the furca by the length of the last joint; the spines of the last thoracic segment were comparatively shorter, the 1st abdominal segment and the anal segment shorter, and the furcal segments only as long as broad (longer than broad in *G. armiger*), and each abdominal segment had a row of pectinations on the posterior border. The saws of the swimming-feet possessed more teeth; the abdomen was not nearly half the length of the cephalothorax, and the whole length of the animal was 5 3 mm. In all these points it differed from the typical *G. armiger*, the size of which reaches only about 3 mm., and justifies its being made into a separate species."

GAIDIUS Gbt. 1895, Bull. Mus. Harvard.

"A good many examples of this genus occurred in the deep-water collections of Dr. Fowler, *e. g* in the bottle marked Meso-plankton 20 (500 to 100 fathoms).

There is no doubt that in the Faeroe Channel there are two kinds of *Gaidius*—one agreeing in every particular with the *Gaidius pungens* of Giesbrecht, the other, a larger species, also differing in the segmentation of the 1st and 2nd feet. *Gaidius pungens* Gbt. has the exopodite of the 1st foot with only two segments and the endopodite of the 2nd foot with only one segment, whereas the northern species has a 3-jointed exopodite of the 1st foot and a two-jointed endopodite of the 2nd foot. There are other minor differences. In size the northern species is much larger, *Gaidius pungens* Gbt. being 4½ mm, as compared with about 3 mm. The *Chirdius tenuispinis* of G O. Sars is the same species, all being characterized by the peculiar series of lamellar appendages of the basipodite of the 4th foot."

PSEUDAETIDEUS ARMATUS Wolfenden.

"Some examples of this species occurred in Dr. Fowler's collection. It was drawn and described (in MSS. only) before the writer became acquainted with the recent work of Prof. G. O Sars, who figured and described the species as *Chiridius armatus*. The writer has published reasons why this generic name should not be used (see Rep. of the Brit. Assoc. 1892, " A proposed Revision of the Subfamily *Aetidinæ*"), as it is not a *Chiridius*."

EUCHIRELLA CARINATA Wolfenden, *op. cit.* p. 366.

" One example of this species, measuring 3 54 mm. in length, was found in Dr. Fowler's collection in the bottle marked 20

"These new species will be described in full, along with the drawings, in the writer's monograph which is in hand."

AMPHIPODA.

I am indebted to the Rev. T. R. R. Stebbing for help in the determination of some of these forms. Only one species occurred in sufficient quantity and with sufficient frequency to enable deductions as to its habitat in the Faeroe Channel being drawn, namely

PARATHEMISTO OBLIVIA Kroyer = *abyssorum* Boeck.

I have already discussed the distribution of this form at some length [1]; to the records there given must be added two stations of the 'National' expedition—N. of the Hebrides, and S.W. of Iceland [2]—and 12 stations along the route of the 'Fram' [3]. Canon Norman also cites Bonnier as having taken it at 950 metres in the Bay of Biscay [4].

It is apparent from the table (p. 119) that the species is a true member of the Mesoplankton in this locality, having been captured in 66 per cent. of the deep hauls; it rises to the surface at midnight, the only occasion out of 26 Epiplankton hauls being at that hour (haul 15 *d*).

CYCLOCARIS GUILELMI Chevreux.

Two specimens of a *Cyclocaris* were obtained in haul 20 *d*, between 500 and 400 fathoms. Mr. Stebbing informs me that they agree undoubtedly with the above species, captured in a net sunk to 600 fathoms near the Lofoten Islands by the 'Princesse Alice' [5], the largest of the six specimens being about 12 mm. in length. My largest specimen, a female, would have measured about 20 mm. if straight.

Another species of this genus, *Cyclocaris tahitensis* Stebbing, was described [6] from a single specimen taken by the 'Challenger' off Tahiti, apparently at the surface [7].

---

[1] Proc. Zool Soc. 1898, pp 583-585.
[2] J Vosseler Amphipoden der Plankton-Expedition, p 80.
[3] F Nansen Norwegian North Polar Expedition Crustacea, by G. O Sars, p. 14
[4] A. M Norman Ann Mag N H (7) v p 131
[5] E. Chevreux Bull Soc Zool France, xxiv. (1899), p. 148
[6] T. R. R Stebbing Chall Rep. Zool, Amphipoda, p 661, pl xvii.
[7] J. Murray Chall. Rep., Summary of Results, p. 1077.

Mr Stebbing points out "that this species has been again figured in great detail by Professor Sars [1], and that Dr. Norman [2] has with almost equal fulness represented his *Cyclocaris faroensis*. In Mr. Stebbing's opinion the differences between the two sets of figures are purely casual, depending on individual or accidental conditions of the specimens examined. Further, while accepting provisionally the distinction between the boreal form and the ' Challenger' *C. tahitensis*, he agrees with the view thus expressed by Dr. Norman, 'so remarkable is the resemblance, that the differences seem scarcely varietal; but I hesitate to unite a form found in the Faroe Channel with one from so distant a locality as Tahiti.' "

Canon Norman does not appear to have known of M. Chevreux's name (which apparently has priority); his specimens were captured by the 'Triton' in the Faeroe Channel in 1882, at a depth of 640 fathoms Professor Sars's specimens were apparently from various depths along the course of the ' Fram,' the smallest specimens at the least depths.

This species (omitting *tahitensis* as specifically distinct) is evidently a Polar and deep-water form.

Tryphana malmi Boeck.

A single specimen, from haul 13 *i*, 100 fathoms to the surface, was identified by Mr. Stebbing. The previous records of its occurrence are: Hardangerfjord, 100 fathoms [3]; from Nansen-fjord to Hardangerfjord [4]; Folgero, Sunde, Foldenfjord, 80 to 100 fathoms [5]. Sars [5] regards *T nordenskioldi* Boeck and *T. boecki* Stebbing as being the males of *T. malmi*. Of these the former [4] was described from the Sofia Expedition as off the Faeroe Islands at 65° N., the latter [6] from 18° 8' N., 30° 5' W., at the surface.

Euthemisto sp. indet.

A number of specimens too much broken for recognition occurred in the haul 15 *d* at midnight.

Euthemisto bispinosa Boeck.

Occurred in 15 *c* (530 to 0 fathoms) and 15 *d* (surface, at midnight). The records of this species were exclusively Arctic, till it was captured by the 'National' expedition in the Sargasso Sea between 218 fathoms and the surface [5]

Euthemisto compressa Goes.

A single specimen at 12 *e* (450 to 320 fathoms) This also was believed to be exclusively an Arctic form, but has now been

[1] F, Nansen · Norwegian North Polar Expedition. G. O. Sars: Crustacea, p 20, pls. ii. & iii
[2] A M Norman · Ann Mag N H (7) v p 197, pl vi
[3] Boeck 'Skandinaviske og Arktiske Amphipoda,' 1872, p. 92.
[4] C Bovallius Vega-Exped Vetensk Iakttag. iv. p 573
[5] Sars Crustacea of Norway, Amphipoda, i p 17 (1890).
[6] T. R R Stebbing Chall Rep. Amphipoda, p 1539.

recorded from the Antarctic region, as well as from the Gulf-Stream proper, the Sargasso Sea, and South Equatorial Drift[1].

EUTHEMISTO LIBELLULA Mandt.

A single specimen in haul 15 d at the surface at midnight. It is widely distributed over the Arctic Seas, but, unlike the two foregoing species, was not taken in southern waters by the 'National.'

SCINA BOREALIS G. O. Sars.

A single specimen from 13 g (465 to 335 fathoms) was accidentally included among the Copepoda sent to Mr Thompson and identified by Mr. A O. Walker. According to Canon Norman[2], the distribution of this species is mesoplanktonic, mostly northern, but also in the Bay of Biscay (960 metres). It reaches to about 80° N.[3]

SCHIZOPODA.

The Schizopoda captured belong exclusively to the Euphausiacea, and are referable to only three species. Several forms which might have been reasonably expected among the captures were absent. A list of the British species with their distribution is given by Canon Norman, in his paper on British Lophogastridæ and Euphausiidæ[4].

THYSANOESSA LONGICAUDATA Kröyer.

A considerable number of specimens of this species were captured · it appeared to be the commonest Schizopod of the Faeroe Channel at the time. The synonymy appears to be *Thysanopoda longicaudata* Kröyer = *Thysanoessa tenera* Sars = *Thysanoessa longicaudata* of Hansen, Norman, Ortmann, &c.

The species ranges from the West Coast of Norway right across to Greenland and into the Labrador current; the 'National'[5] ceased to take it (after almost daily captures up to that moment) from the date of entering the warm water of the Gulf-Stream ('Florida-strom'). Sars[6], who described the species from deep water in the Varanger Fjord, records it also as from the surface at four stations between Norway and Jan Mayen on the cruise of the 'Vöringen'[7]. It appears, therefore, to be essentially a cold-water species, an Arctic type-form, and was captured by the 'Fram'[8]

It has, however, been recorded twice from British coasts[9].

[1] Vosseler Amphipoden der Plankton-Expedition, p 86.
[2] A M Norman Ann. Mag. N. H (7) v. p 135.
[3] F. Nansen, *op cit* p 19
[4] A Ortmann Ann Mag. Nat Hist. (6) ix. p. 454.
[5] A Ortmann 'Decapoden und Schizopoden der Plankton-Expedition,' p 14.
[6] G O Sars · Forhandlinger Videnskabs-Selskabet (Christiania), 1882, no 18, p 53.
[7] G. O Sars Norwegian North Atlantic Expedition (Crustacea), pt ii p. 13.
[8] F. Nansen Norwegian North Polar Expedition G. O Sars Crustacea, p 14
[9] A. M Norman Ann Mag. Nat. Hist (6) ix. p. 463, and the papers there cited.

Once it occurred in enormous quantity in St. Andrew's Bay in company with *Nyctiphanes norvegica*, once at Redcar with a similar swarm of *Euthemisto compressa*, the latter being also an Arctic type-form [1]. In both these cases it is probable that the creatures had been driven down the North Sea by a strong southerly current, in the manner which I have already suggested [2] for *Parathemisto oblivia* ; and it has therefore no more right to be regarded as a " British " species than an occasional *Velella* or *Ianthina* brought up by the North Atlantic Drift to our shores. According to Ortmann (*op cit*), the 'National' hauls gave no indication of the vertical distribution of this species.

It will appear from the table (p. 119) that the ' Research ' was more fortunate, and the hauls point to its having a distinct preference for the mesoplankton in the Faeroe Channel. Like (at any rate some) other mesoplanktonic species, it rises to the surface at night. Specimens with adult characters were captured in 19 per cent of epiplankton hauls, but in 66 per cent. of mesoplankton hauls. On the other hand, larval and post-larval stages, apparently referable to this species, were obtained in 38 per cent. of epiplankton hauls, but only in one mesoplankton haul, and that one terminating near the 100 fathoms. The species, therefore, appears to be epiplanktonic when young, mesoplanktonic when adult, so far as these observations go and in the Faeroe Channel at this time of year   In seeking deeper (colder) water in this locality, it follows what appears to be the practice of other Arctic type-forms when they meet the warmer water of the North Atlantic Drift. That this was not apparent from the results of the 'National' is probably due to the fact that from the Hebrides almost up to the moment of coming into the Gulf-Stream the vessel was in far colder surface-water than that of the Faeroe Channel in summer

The larvæ mentioned above ranged from an early *Calyptopis* stage up to the adult condition. It was not, of course, possible to derive them all with certainty from *Thysanoessa longicaudata* ; but the majority may be safely referred to this species, not only because the adults captured were far in excess of any other Euphausid, but also because the larvæ could be traced gradually through successive stages back to the *Calyptopis*. The metamorphoses of this species follow the lines indicated by Sars [3] for *Nyctiphanes*, *Euphausia*, and *Thysanopoda*

As Paul Mayer [4] has shown, the spination of the telson of Malacostracan larvæ yields a character important both for phylogeny and for diagnosis. It has not as yet, I think, been pointed out that the condition of the telson in Euphausiidæ affords a further argument for the view maintained by Boas [5] and others,

[1] C Chun ' Beziehungen zwischen dem arktischen und antarktischen Plankton,' Stuttgart, 1897, 8vo, p. 30
[2] Proc Zool Soc 1898, p 583
[3] G O Sars Chall Rep Zool. xiii. (Schizopoda)
[4] P Mayer Jenaische Zeitschrift, xi (1877), p 246 *et seqq*
[5] J E V. Boas: Morphologisches Jahrbuch, viii p 485

that this family takes its origin very near to the root of the Decapodan stem, and that it has far closer affinities with the latter than with the Mysidæ. In *Nyctiphanes*[1] and *Euphausia*[2], and possibly in other genera also, the youngest *Calyptopis*-larvæ show seven spines on each side of the telson; unlike all other Schizopoda, so far as is known, except perhaps *Lophogaster*, they are thus in absolute accord with the "ursprungliche Borstenzahl $7+7$" which Mayer attributes to the primitive Macruran and Brachyuran. In *Euphausia, Nyctiphanes, Thysanopoda,* and *Nematoscelis* according to Sars (*op. cit.*), and in *Thysanoessa,* the number is increased at later stages by a median terminal spine, which, like the others, is jointed to the telson. Accepting Mayer's enumeration of the spines from the middle line outwards, and styling the median azygos spine of the Euphausiidæ as 0,— spines 7 are found in the adult *Thysanoessa* about one-third of the length of the telson from the root; spines 6 at about two-thirds of its length from the root; spines 5 are lost; spines 4 persist as the large lateral jointed spines near the end of the adult telson[3]; and spines 3, 2, 1, 0 disappear altogether in the course of development. On page 131, I have illustrated four stages in this reduction omitted by Sars, of which fig 15 does not quite bear out his description · these show the disappearance of the median spine 0, and the commencement of a new *unjointed* growth of the telson backwards, to form the lanceolate tip of the adult. The character of the telson and the presence of this median spine will apparently form a good criterion for the separation of Euphausidan larvæ (at stages later than the Meta-nauplius) from other Schizopodan and from Decapodan larvæ.

The earliest *Calyptopis*-larvæ captured by the 'Research' resembled closely those figured by Sars (*op. cit.*) for other genera, except for the facts that the carapace was much more globular anteriorly and was devoid of spines or processes.

NYCTIPHANES NORVEGICA M. Sars.

This form was captured on only six occasions   Although a North Atlantic type, it is not an essentially Arctic type like *Thysanoessa longicaudata* . it is of constant occurrence in certain localities on our own coasts, and has been recorded from as far south as Portugal. The various records of its occurrence are cited by Canon Norman[4], but unfortunately the size of the individuals and the depth from which they were derived are only rarely noted. I am informed by Sir John Murray that, in his experience, large adult specimens are taken only in deep water.

---

[1] G O. Sars · Chall. Rep Zool., xiii Schizopoda, pl. xxvii fig. 6.
[2] C. Claus Untersuch. Crustaceen-Systems, pl 1 fig 2, Wien, 1876, 4to
[3] With regard to these, Boas (*op. cit* p 523, note 5) has suggested that they may be homologous with the long caudal appendages of *Nebalia* and many Phyllopods This possibility is rendered considerably more remote by their being merely two persistent spines out of a series which is not represented in the forms cited by him
[4] A M. Norman Ann. Mag Nat. Hist (6) ix. pp 459–460 (1892)

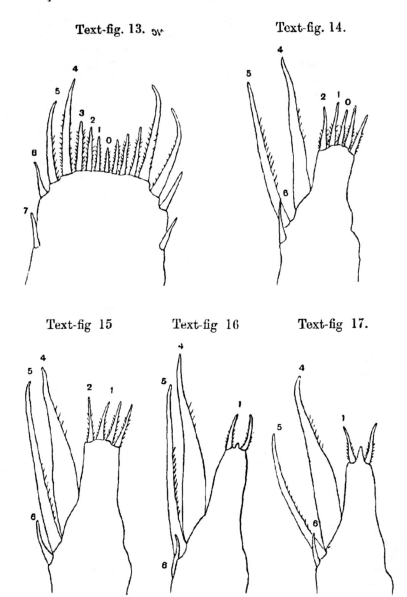

Telsons of larvæ attributed to *Thysanoessa longicaudata*, showing reduction of the
primitive seven pairs of spines and formation of the median unjointed spine
of the telson

Fig. 13   Early *Calyptopis*, 1 5 mm long
   ,, 14   *Furcilia*, 4 5 mm. long
   ,, 15   *Cyrtopia*, 5 mm long
   ,, 16   Late *Cyrtopia*, 5 mm long.
   ,, 17   4 mm long

The same distribution was noted by Vallentin and Cunningham [1] —"The adult, so far as our information allows of a decision, lives on the bottom, and never swims far from the ground [90–95 fathoms in this instance], while the young, up to half or three-quarters the size of the adult, occur abundantly at the very surface and at all intermediate depths. As mentioned above, Mr. Murray found swarms of individuals at the surface in the Faroe Channel, but none of these were full-grown, and very few more than half the adult size."

I have no doubt that this generalization will prove true for greater depths : I took adult specimens, over 35 mm. in length, only between 350–220 fathoms, 400–300 fathoms, 500–400 fathoms : the remaining specimens varied from 9 to 17 mm. in length.   In other words, *Nyctiphanes norvegica* is apparently mesoplanktonic when adult.

A few larvæ, larger for their stage of development than those attributed to *Thysanoessa*, were taken at the surface, and may perhaps belong to *Nyctiphanes* : they have not been included in the tables.

THYSANOPODA MICROPHTHALMA Ortmann.   (? = *Thysanopoda microphthalma* G. O. Sars)

Three specimens, recognizable as young forms by the character of the second maxilla and gills, and by the spination of the telson, of about eight, twelve, and fourteen mm. in length, appear to be referable to the same species as specimens recorded in quantity by the 'National' in 60° 3′ N , 27° 0′ W., at a probable depth of between 218 and 328 fathoms.   These were referred by Ortmann [2] to *Thysanopoda microphthalma* of Sars [3], a species founded on two specimens from the *surface* at 26° 21′ N., 33° 37′ W , and 7° N , 23° W. respectively.   The identity of the 'National' specimens with those described by Sars seems to me rather doubtful firstly, because it is not very likely that a rare form such as this should occur as adult both at the surface near the Equator and also at 218–328 fathoms in the Greenland Sea, or at 500–400 fathoms in the yet colder water of the Faeroe Channel ; secondly, because Ortmann himself indicates some points of difference between his specimens and those of Sars.   My own specimens agree with Ortmann's figure, and differ from Sars's description, in the shape of the antennal scale, and in the absence of a spine from the second joint of the first antenna.   The telson was not hispid, probably owing to immaturity; the eye was somewhat flatter than in Ortmann's figure, and showed slight signs of a constriction such as is characteristic of *Thysanoessa*.   The matter cannot be settled in default of further specimens, owing to the fact that Sars gave only a woodcut of the entire animal, and no figures of the detailed anatomy.

---

[1] R Vallentin & J T Cunningham Quart Journ Micr Sci xxviii pp 325–6
[2] A Ortmann 'Decapoden und Schizopoden der Plankton-Expedition,' p 9
[3] G O. Sars Chall Rep Zool , xiii Schizopoda, p 106

1903]   133

Of the three Research specimens of this species two came
from the Mesoplankton, one from a haul of 480 to 0 fathoms
no examples were captured at the surface unless some
of the larvae attributed to Thysanoessa belonged to this species,
this is unlikely, because in that case the small size
of the eyes would probably have betrayed them

CPSIA information can be obtained at www.ICGtesting.com
Printed in the USA
BVOW01s1050211014

371687BV00020B/632/P